Avidly Reads PASSAGES

Avidly Reads

General Editors: Sarah Mesle and Sarah Blackwood

A series of short books about how culture makes us feel.

Avidly Reads Theory
Jordan Alexander Stein

Avidly Reads Making Out
Kathryn Bond Stockton

Avidly Reads Board Games
Eric Thurm

Avidly Reads Passages
Michelle D. Commander

Passages

MICHELLE D. COMMANDER

NEW YORK UNIVERSITY PRESS *New York*

NEW YORK UNIVERSITY PRESS
New York
www.nyupress.org

© 2021 by New York University
All rights reserved

Lucille Clifton, "i am accused of tending to the past" from *The Collected Poems of Lucille Clifton*. Copyright © 1991 by Lucille Clifton. Reprinted with the permission of The Permissions Company, LLC on behalf of BOA Editions, Ltd., boaeditions.org.

References to Internet websites (URLs) were accurate at the time of writing. Neither the author nor New York University Press is responsible for URLs that may have expired or changed since the manuscript was prepared.

Cataloging in Publication Data is available from the publisher.
ISBN 9781479806164 (hardcover)
ISBN 9781479806171 (paperback)
ISBN 9781479806133 consumer ebook)
ISBN 9781479806188 (library ebook)

New York University Press books are printed on acid-free paper, and their binding materials are chosen for strength and durability. We strive to use environmentally responsible suppliers and materials to the greatest extent possible in publishing our books.

Manufactured in the United States of America

10 9 8 7 6 5 4 3 2 1

Also available as an ebook

i am accused of tending to the past
as if i made it,
as if i sculpted it
with my own hands. i did not.
this past was waiting for me
when i came,
a monstrous unnamed baby,
and i with my mother's itch
took it to breast
and named it
History.
she is more human now,
learning languages everyday,
remembering faces, names and dates.
when she is strong enough to travel
on her own, beware, she will.

—Lucille Clifton, "i am accused of tending to the past"

Contents

Preface — xi

1. Ship — 1

2. Train — 29

3. Automobile — 65

4. Bus — 105

Coda: Passages — 135

Acknowledgments — 145

Bibliography — 147

About the Author — 151

Preface

On a summer trip home in the early 2000s, I stopped at a gas station in Brunswick, Georgia. I plugged the nozzle into the gas tank and turned to walk toward the store. A sudden, loud growl from the engine of an ancient pickup truck caught my ear, and I paused to watch as an enormous Confederate flag, extending the length of the truck's bed, billowed in the air.

Instinctively, I pivoted to stick closer to my car. As the driver pulled up to a neighboring pump between the store and me, I calculated my options. Could I dodge him if I moved quickly enough toward the entrance? The middle-aged white man slumped out of his truck while, seconds too late to avoid his path, I advanced. I had tried to slow my pace to the door, but the man held it for me, allowing me to enter before him. He asked, "How are you doing, ma'am," his comportment steeped in a kind of feigned southern gentility that contrasted with, but certainly did not absolve him of, the scene that he had created by hoisting from his vehicle the most prominent symbol of southern racism, white supremacist and nationalist bigotry, and contempt for Black life and breath. I was only able to muster an obligatory, "Thanks. Fine and you?" in response, but I did not await an answer. I rushed into the restroom instead.

Back on the road, I realized that just as I did not truly care how the man was feeling though I asked, he too might not have been sincere in his politeness, only addressing me to test whether his spectacle and "good old boy" performance had *moved me* in some way. As painful as it is to admit, his performance did affect me, did partially constrain me. I did not freeze completely during the momentary interaction; but my heart palpitated, and a sudden tingle trickled up the back of my neck and down the length of my arms, besetting me with panic about what might have happened if I did not retreat.

As an African American native of the South, my fear of these interactions compels me to drive sometimes slowly and sometimes quickly through certain towns. Of course, I also travel through the world with the joy and calm that come along with holiday retreats from the pressures of everyday life. More often, though, a sense that one ought to be hypervigilant often accompanies African Americans as we negotiate the expanse of sky, highway, and sea, endeavoring to get from one place to another. As Christina Sharpe notes in *In the Wake: On Blackness and Being* about the very real trepidation, dehumanization, and lack of care that haunts Black people in the afterlife of slavery, "Living in the wake means living the history and present of terror, from slavery to the present, as the ground of our everyday Black existence; living the historically and geographically dis/continuous but always present and endlessly reinvigorated brutality in, and on, our bodies while even as that terror is visited on our bodies the realities of that terror are erased" (15).

It's not just the one man at the gas station who moves me, restricts me. The legacy of white supremacy in its many relentless forms torments and dispossesses Black people and seeks to keep us in our places. Its persistence prompts me to reflect on the question of whether the South's (and America's) sordid entanglements with racism and its perpetually renovated restrictions on Black movement will forever suffuse the fascinatingly beautiful and grotesque landscape in which I grew and thus cannot help but love.

Avidly Reads Passages ruminates on this enduring aspect of slavery's complex aftermath. It does so through engagements with my familial histories and a wealth of other relevant cultural materials. Long before I gained the affective language to describe the ways that my family, other people of African descent, and I experienced the limitations of and possibilities for our mobility, I very much understood the inherent precariousness attached to many of our movements. This book considers how the promises of literal and figurative flight above and across the United States' contentious social and political terrains continue to pique and sustain the Black imagination.

I retell this history using my beloved home of Lower Richland County, South Carolina, as a point of return and focus. My personal accounts are complemented by a range of evidences: narratives of slavery, travel accounts, major events in civil rights history, and genealogy to account for the history of Black passages in new and, hopefully, resonant ways.

The slave ship compelled the inauguration of African American identity against these turbulent shores, and so that is the mode of transport with which I begin. Each chapter focuses on the rise of subsequent forms of transport—the train, the automobile, the bus—that became crucial to the development of American culture, sense of upward mobility, and ascent into particular kinds of modernity. And I place these forms alongside other passages: a range of laws passed over the course of more than two centuries that regulate and control the movements of African Americans.

But like the complicated history of the African American experience writ large, my chapters are not always temporally or narratively linear. For my enslaved family, travel was alternately an incredible cruelty and a longed-for possibility; where they lived could be a prison or a haven. You will find in my chapters different kinds of transportation meeting each other unexpectedly: swamps enabling the freedom that trains could not, for instance, or ships (military ones, this time) indirectly enabling automobiles. But this is because, in the southern Black history I tell, progress is uneven, and our passages are too.

1

SHIP

> Sails flashing to the wind like weapons,
> sharks following the moans the fever and the dying;
> horror the corposant and compass rose.
>
> Middle Passage:
>   voyage through death
>   to life upon these shores.
> —Robert Hayden, *Middle Passage*

Packed tightly into ships pointed west to places unknown, they saw and felt the unimaginable. Curiously pale-faced humans at their worst: kidnapping, shoving, packing, surveilling, shouting, and violating. And another set, faces dark like their own: beautiful, strong, stoic, yet afraid. As victims and witnesses, the African captives had been ripped from near and distant lands. Having already suffered in innumerable ways, they endeavored to breathe, to live. There was moaning and crying. Bursts of shouting, struggling, rebelling, pleading, fighting back, and, yes, giving up.

    Untold numbers jumped defiantly into the surf, children in their grasp. How eager they were to spiritually ascend.

For those who remained, the heat and hunger became acute. There was confusion and desperation. Sickness, lack of drink, and breathlessness. A thick, ghastly stench stalled in the air. Darkness. The ship rocked gently in fair weather, adding a bitter lull to the suffering, its sway not unlike a mother comforting her young. With abruptness, tempestuous winds and walls of waves pushed up against and tilted the ship. Its human cargo, which had been irreverently tucked underneath, slid at awkward angles, their skin pinched and ripped off as they scraped against metal chains. The captives' stomachs became unnerved with seasickness as their bodies jerked. Bile and bowels passed everywhere. Did they suspect the hell on earth that awaited? Fate had placed them in close proximity to other dark bodies, chained and strange and dying. Together, their sonic turmoil produced a dissonant harmony that floated across the Atlantic for weeks, "the whole a scene of horror almost inconceivable" (Equiano 38). The Middle Passage: an oceanic pathway of despair, dispossession, and endings. Impossibly sorrowful, fateful beginnings.

***

There is a lot that I don't know about my family's history, but the one thing I know for sure is this: my ancestors came by ship. And many survived for a time. Like the estimated four hundred thousand or so captives transported to North America during the slave trade, they had been sold and stolen from inland regions of West and Central Africa and eventually forced into the suffocating slave-castle dungeons that dotted the coastline. Some weeks later, those who endured the atrocious conditions were tightly packed once more into slave ships en route through the Middle Passage and toward disembarkation points in the Americas and the Caribbean.

It was a disorienting voyage for the captives, as they "lacked a culture of maritime travel, and the ship produced in them an experience of motion without discernible direction or destination" (Smallwood 122). This shipping, the dehumanizing process undertaken to first dislocate and then begin stripping Africans of their agency, rendered them mere objects on whom their enslavers' will would be done.

In 1788, centuries into the slave trade, the Plymouth Committee of the Society for Effecting the Abolition of the Slave Trade in England began distributing the image of the slave ship *Brookes*. The *Brookes* had been permitted to carry 454 African slaves, by allowing a space of six feet (1.8 meters) by one foot four inches (0.41 meters) to each man; five feet ten inches (1.78 meters) by one foot four inches (0.41 meters) to each woman, and five feet (1.5 meters) by one foot two inches (0.36 meters) to each child. On some voyages, the *Brookes* illegally carried upward of six hundred captive Africans at once. This startling image and related versions were shared widely in pamphlets, books, and other antislavery propaganda to give the public a visual sense of the

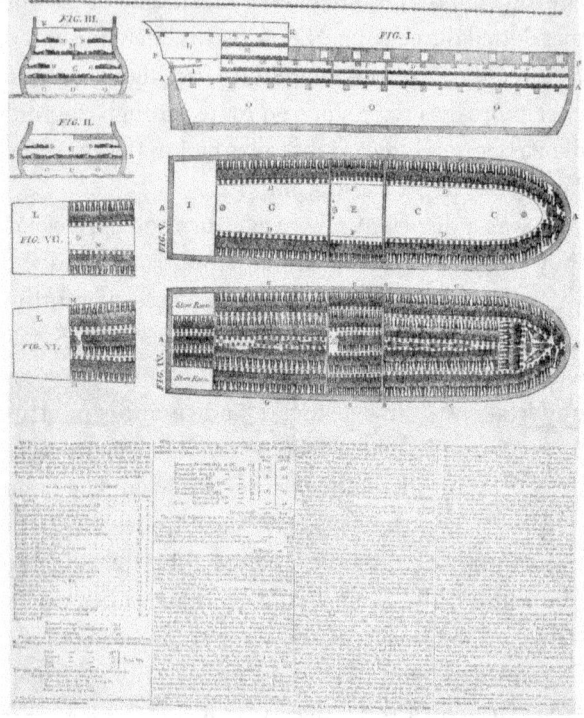

Brookes ship diagram. (Thomas Clarkson, "Description of a Slave Ship," *The History of the Rise, Progress, and Accomplishment of the Abolition of the African Slave-Trade by the British Parliament* [London, 1808], www.bl.uk/collection-items/diagram-of-the-brookes-slave-ship)

appalling nature of the slave trade. The imagery continues to circulate today as a horrible kind of witness.

As a transatlantic slave ship icon, the *Brookes* diagram features intricate detail in its antislavery iteration and evokes a number of reactions from viewers. There is the sense of unease at the subject of slavery itself. At first glance, one notices the ways that human beings are carefully packed and shackled into the ships. Upon even closer inspection, perhaps prompted by the thought of *how* something so brutally inhumane and so unjust could have ever happened on a transnational scale and across centuries, one comes to grips with the realization that this method was driven by financial calculation. The packing of the slave ship was a regulated, strategic, and mundane aspect of the trade. That is but one of its horrors.

While very few first-person accounts of the Middle Passage exist from those who experienced the journey as captives, a major voice survives.

Witness 1

Olaudah Equiano's account *The Interesting Narrative of the Life of Olaudah Equiano; or, Gustavus Vassa, the African* offers some insight. In 1789, Equiano published his narrative to chronicle the circumstances leading up to the kidnapping of himself and his sister into slavery, their permanent separation from each other, and Equiano's life through increasingly more brutal forms of slavery as a victim and witness, including his service to captains of slave ships and British navy vessels. Equiano—who famously inquires about his and his fellow captives' fates, "What was to be done with us?"—recalls the sensory excesses of the slave ship hold,

> The closeness of the place, and the heat of the climate, added to the number in the ship, which was so crowded that each had scarcely room to turn himself, almost suffocated us. This produced copious perspirations, so that the air soon became unfit for respiration, from a variety of loathsome smells, and brought on a sickness among the slaves, of which many died, thus falling victims to the improvident avarice, as I may call it, of their purchasers. This wretched situation was again aggravated by the galling of the chains, now become insupportable; and the filth of the necessary tubs, into which the children often fell, and were almost suffocated. (37–38)

And then there are those who observed the captives on their passage but failed to intervene.

Witness 2

In 1788, Alexander Falconbridge, a British surgeon, slaver, and later an abolitionist, methodically reported about the appalling conditions that he observed aboard slave ships in *An Account of the Slave Trade on the Coast of Africa.* Note the detached manner in which he, who for some time supported the trade firsthand in all of its dehumanizing ways, characterizes the conditions under which African captives suffered:

> [The captives] are frequently stowed so close, as to admit of no other posture than lying on their sides. Neither will the height between decks, unless directly under the grating, permit them the indulgence of an erect posture; especially where there are platforms, which is generally the case. These platforms are a kind of shelf, about eight or nine feet in breadth, extending from the side of the ship towards the center. They are placed nearly midway between the decks, at the distance of two or three feet from each deck. Upon these the Negroes are stowed in the same manner as they are on the deck underneath. . . .
>
> As very few of the Negroes can so far [handle] the loss of their liberty and the hardships they endure, they are ever on the watch to take advantage of the least negligence in their oppressors. Insurrections are frequently the consequence; which are seldom expressed without much bloodshed. Sometimes these are successful and the whole ship's company is cut off. They are likewise always ready to seize every opportunity for committing some acts of desperation to free themselves from their

> miserable state and notwithstanding the restraints which are laid, they often succeed. (20, 30)

Contemptuously separated from kith and kin during subsequent passages via intra-American voyages and/or agonizing sales transactions from southern auction blocks, my ancestors were unjustly shipped and sentenced to new lives under the inhumaneness of chattel slavery. With their movements strategically controlled, they would go on to move and be moved an untold number of times, remaking their lives at nearly every turn.

* * *

One of these turns eventually brought my ancestors to the lower portion of Richland County, South Carolina. Lower Richland has been the site of quite a few incorporated and unincorporated towns over the years. I grew up mostly in Eastover and the eastern outskirts of Columbia, while my closest-related known kin in Lower Richland have lived across the region in Hopkins, Gadsden, Wateree, and due east in St. Matthews. Other South Carolina relatives live in Beaufort and Colleton Counties, the descendants of my great-uncle, his Gullah-Geechee wife, and their children. Those who left South Carolina moved by themselves or with their immediate families to Detroit, Memphis, New York City, and Philadelphia.

For much of my childhood, my immediate family and I lived on a woodsy road along a quarter-mile stretch of quaint homes that face a wall of giant pine trees. It is a forest full of trees so tall and so ancient that their crowns appear to touch the sky.

Whenever we traveled using the back way out of the neighborhood, choosing Bluff Road over Garners Ferry Road to avoid traffic jams, we crossed the railroad tracks, alongside which lies an endless emerald pathway. I imagine movement in this clearing; it is a kind of green screen on which my imagination, prompted by recollections of what I have gleaned about the area's history in the archives, actively conjures up scenes of long-lost peoples rebelling in small and substantial ways and loving one another with abandon. I marvel at their ceaseless determination to harness flight and be free. From here, in slavery's *wake*, I pause and give reverence to the living and to the dead.

In the 1700s, the Congaree, Wateree, and Cherokee peoples lived around Mill Creek, where I spent a fair share of my childhood living in an adjacent subdivision centuries later. Very little is recorded in studies about the area regarding the Native American population, whose sacred lands have been fouled by a series of seemingly unending atrocities, including battles for their land and resources and then-fatal epidemic catastrophes brought on by smallpox and other infectious diseases.

In 1739, South Carolina's Company of Rangers was founded to protect the European settlers from possible ambush by the indigenous communities. The indigenous had obvious historical reasons for alarm, given that they were being moved to the fringes of the sacred lands on which they lived and cultivated harvest. Two centuries prior in the spring of 1540, Hernando De Soto and his army of six hundred conquistadors passed through the Congaree region in search of gold and other treasures in the Cofitachequi chiefdom, where they ransacked and looted settlements and kidnapped the chieftainess, forcing her to lead them to precious trinkets and artifacts. The British explorer John Lawson's 1709 travel account, entitled *A New Voyage to Carolina*, also references the Congaree, noting their kind dispositions, their agricultural acumen, the suitability of the land for plantations, and the British settlers' curious engagements with the Congaree, namely, the revolting reasons they listed for taking the Congaree girls and women as "bedfellows."

European immigrants and other white settlers who had lived throughout the upper South arrived in Lower Richland beginning in the 1700s. Tracking through old records, I find the surnames of those listed as the earliest settlers. Among the names on land plat maps, wills and estate records, and bills of sale are many that *belong* to my family and many of the other Black folks with whom I was raised: the Goodwyns/Goodwins, Myers, Tuckers, Taylors, and Howells. It was one thing to be generally aware of how we got our names. It was quite another to hold a significant piece of the centuries-long history in my hands . . . to read a summary of the land and rapacious slavery speculation that rendered the violent displacement of my ancestors from their African homelands as logical, compulsory. Our names, indeed, are a curious inheritance.

In the decades after the initial settlement in Lower Richland, Africans were captured and sold in increasing numbers to toil as human labor on the region's indigo and cotton plantations. For some time, the number of enslaved persons outnumbered the European population, a fact that fomented anxiety in the Europeans and probably caused them to act out violently as they attempted to maintain supremacy. In 1739, Royal Governor Robert Johnson devised a plan to encourage European migration to the area from England, Germany, Switzerland, and Holland to help increase the white population. More white people, they thought, would bolster their efforts to defend themselves against the justifiably uncooperative Native American communities as well as to tamp down the possibility of resistance and rebellion by the quickly growing enslaved population. I wonder: were my ancestors among those they feared?

European enslavers and lawmakers, who had forcibly brought Africans to this land, also aimed to legislate the restriction of enslaved people's movement. Their minds were still on the recent Stono Rebellion (1739), which had taught them a significant lesson about the swiftness with which their control could be turned upside down. During this bloody insurrection, a fugitive band of Konoglese enslaved men had marched forthrightly from their respective plantations in the South Carolina Lowcountry, recruiting some sixty counterparts along the way as they battled with white militias. They were determined to migrate to freedom in Spanish Florida's free Black settlement Gracia Real de Saint Teresa de Mosé (Fort Mose). Though most of the Kongolese insurrectionists did not successfully make it to freedom and were either killed or sold to plantation owners in the Caribbean for the murderous uprising, their resolute posture demonstrated that enslaved people would continue to protest their captivity by collectively and forcibly reclaiming the right to their own mobility. This insurgent spirit gave pause to enslavers in South Carolina who were ultimately concerned with protecting their own lives.

By 1740, thirty-nine thousand people of African descent and twenty thousand Europeans lived all over Richland County. In response to this very common, inverted dynamic in the early colonies, increasing instances of indirect and direct forms of resistance by the enslaved, and other moments of insurrection across the Atlantic world, South Carolina lawmakers passed the Act for the Better Ordering and Governing Negroes and Other Slaves in This Province in 1740. The act offered detailed guidelines for the regulation of slavery, encoding into the law all aspects of the lives of those "deemed absolute slaves" whether they were "Negroes, Indians, mulattoes, or mestizos" (South Carolina 1).

The laws therein placed restrictions that ranged from enslaved peoples' ability to travel within and outside the plantations on which they labored, the quality of their dress, their access to formal education, and their ability to convene with other enslaved peoples to one of the most significant, consequential, and far-reaching aspects of the statutes: the outlining of the ways that the enslaved (and their descendants) were expected to comport themselves as subjects to *all* white people. The fifth statute is especially vivid in its description of how white-supremacist philosophies informed the American colony's order: "And it shall be further enacted by the authority aforesaid, That if any slave who shall be out of the house or plantation where such slave shall live, or shall be usually employed, or without some white person in company with such slave, shall refuse to submit or undergo the examination of any white person, it shall be lawful for any such white person to pursue, apprehend, and moderately correct such slave; and if any such slave shall assault and [strike] such white person, such slave may be lawfully killed" (South Carolina 3). Along with the expectation of submission came the deputizing of white people from whom the incessant harassment of enslaved people often led to violent interactions and even death.

Encoded in South Carolina's 1740 ordinances, too, is evidence of the roots of white fear and paranoia of the *other*, which are merely racist white people's bogeyman projections of their own avariciousness, propensity to plunder lands and cultures, and ruthless reactions to enslaved people's attempts to govern their own lives.

This long-standing psychological torture and gaslighting is why I am unashamed to admit that I marvel at recorded instances of resistance. When I imagine the torment and pain heaped on enslaved people by their enslavers or their representatives within the slaveholding region's geography of containment, I long for counternarratives. That is, I want to read and luxuriate in stories of Black intransigence and vengeance either unearthed and published by historians or stumbled on in the archives via a random diary entry or letter between white family members. I am exceedingly heartened by enslaved people's will to survive. Their defiant postures and their organizing across cultural differences and geographic spaces are a balm.

Philosophically, their fugitivity offers instruction for negotiating our own times.

* * *

Scholars and genealogists alike find that scouring through the archives of slavery brings moments of exhilaration and sheer disappointment. When working on assuaging a curiosity in my familial lineage, I often come so close to an answer about an ancestor, when a misspelled name, missing record, or some other brick wall abruptly halts my quest to make sense of, say, the 1860 slave schedules alongside the hastily taken 1870 census. While nearly anyone conducting genealogical research will encounter gaps in historical logic and other curiosities, I am all too often dismayed that a person can be lost to time. The notion that a person—a precious life—could be relegated to an unnamed, common numerical annotation in an enslaver's estate ledger alongside livestock or other property always boggles my mind, no matter how often I encounter these documents in the archive.

The Lower Richland enslaver Wright Denley's 1850 slave schedule indicates that a five-year-old enslaved girl was in his possession at the time that the census was recorded. I was ecstatic when this line item correlated with the appearance of my then twenty-five-year-old third great-grandmother, Letty Richardson, and her family in the 1870 census. I have no family Bible or passed-on story that arms me with many other names to cross-check, only a local historian's confirmation that one of my maternal ancestral lines descends from people who once occupied that particular place. Perhaps some aspect of Letty's countenance is written on my own. Or maybe she is in my pigeon-toed, flat-footed stride, in my mad professorial gesticulations as I grasp for a word during a lecture or a heated debate, or in my proclivity for not suffering fools.

As is the case for most African Americans whose ancestors were enslaved in what is now the United States, my family possesses no precious fading photos or gilded-framed daguerreotypes. We have not seen intimate letters between antebellum family members or lovers. Very few well-marked, preserved gravesites for the enslaved remain to account for their being. In fact, contemporary land speculators in the midst of digging up the earth for a new housing subdivision or strip mall are sometimes surprised by their construction workers' unwitting uncovering of slave burial grounds. Such findings often result in the reburial of the remains elsewhere or, more rarely, a complete construction stoppage.

With so many unweaveable pieces, it becomes difficult to stitch together a solid understanding of my family's early history in Lower Richland, let alone their individual dreams and actual life experiences—how they moved or didn't, how they felt about leaving or staying. The not-knowing does, however, have an at once frustrating and comforting way of rendering nearly every well-documented story about slavery as one that could have been experienced by my enslaved ancestors, as they are many and as we, their heirs, are far-flung across the Atlantic world.

The feeling that I am attempting to describe here is not simply about belated nostalgia or wistful longings but the very real acknowledgment of how slavery created and helped sustain a philosophy of white supremacy that has permeated our present moment. As Stephanie M. H. Camp notes about slavery's principles of restraint in *Closer to Freedom: Enslaved Women and Everyday Resistance in the Plantation South*, "Enslaved people in the nineteenth century were trapped in more than an exploitative labor relation; they were the captive losers in a battle for power that had begun centuries earlier in the Atlantic maritime world. Enslavement in the American South meant cultural alienation, reduction to the status of property. . . . It entailed the strictest control of the physical and social mobility of enslaved people" (12). The most infamous of slave revolts affected laws throughout the South as well as the ways that white people viewed the bodies of enslaved people, assigning value in intentional and arbitrary ways. The persistence of white surveillance and restrictions on Black movement aimed to curb rebellion and maintain the investments of all those who benefited, directly or indirectly, from the institution. Enslavers' stories about Black belligerence abounded and spread quickly across the South, as did some white people's belated worries that rebellious behavior among the enslaved was caused by their owners' abhorrent treatment.

With the wealth of narratives about the violent atrocities that attended the institution of slavery actually in the record (we can only speculate about what might have been excised), it is difficult to resist becoming overwhelmed with grief and rage in my wonderment at how my enslaved ancestors and their counterparts dealt with the constant threat of sexual abuse and other physical and psychic violations. Based on the household compositions cataloged by the census collectors in the immediate postbellum period, I imagine that my enslaved kin had spent their lives determined to establish surrogate families to still the emotional turmoil that came along with biological family separations; loved ones dying premature deaths from yellow fever, infections, or minor illnesses that could have been prevented and/or cured with the medical treatment of the day; and fatigue from unrelenting hours spent toiling in the unforgiving South Carolina sun. With the sounds of agony induced by the overseers' mocking threats and the crisp cracks of their whips against and across bodies serving as a horrific soundtrack, the enslaved laborers must have been both bone tired and incensed. How did they rest?

* * *

In the afterlife, we descendants of enslaved Africans are left to envisage our foreparents' joys and their strivings for freedom. I grew up without a true awareness of the history of the land on which we lived, so my aghastness at many elements of the region's history is indeed belated. My scholarly interests in transatlantic slavery exposed some embarrassing gaps in my knowledge of who I am and from whence I came. By graduate school, I found myself in an anxious rush to find out everything possible.

I had seemingly always been aware that my maternal great-grandparents, born in the so-called Gilded Age, had been manual laborers, sharecroppers, and farmers on their own and rented plots of land. My grandmother and her siblings had been taught skills that equipped them to make the earth work for themselves. They fed their families by planting crops and raising livestock. Ever resourceful, they traded bunches of collard greens, tomatoes, and baskets of beans with one another for freshly butchered beef and pork, hand-made sausages, fried pork skins, and cracklins. This bartering system carried on into my childhood.

I have a clear recollection of my grandmother's garden in her backyard in Eastover, one that she, my grandfather, and their children had tended over the years. Large, bountiful pecan and plum trees stood adjacent to the fertile plot of land. The time that Grandma Isabell spent cultivating her garden was the only occasion that she let her holy guard down. As a devout Christian woman whose usual outfits consisted of dresses, skirts, and blouses, she only ever broke form to wear pants when she was working in the garden or tending to her roses and hydrangeas in the front yard. When I lived with her during my preschool years, I would often watch her from an open kitchen window. She spent much of her time slightly bent down over the soil, using her hoe or shovel to tend to each neatly laid row.

Grandma did not work quietly: she had a perpetual tune of a Christian hymn in her throat and a verbalized praise to Jesus for his goodness and mercy on the tip of her tongue. While I understood from her and my mother that serious gardening had been passed down in the family for generations, there was almost total silence about slavery throughout my childhood. The memories from generations back must have felt too close and too painful to mention and therefore tucked away, perhaps given over to a higher power, never to be uttered again.

The first century of slavery's aftermath in the United States undoubtedly was enough to contend with: Black codes, white domestic terrorist groups that aimed to maintain the old order, segregated facilities, poor work wages, and stock-market crashes. The absence of familial oral testimony from the era of slavery meant that we lived among marked and unmarked vestiges of slavery along Lower Richland's country roads, unaware of the powerful, painful, and utterly remarkable historical narratives in our own literal and figurative backyards.

As an older child living in Mill Creek with my parents, I was given permission to roam with friends all day on most Saturdays. Our favorite pastime was racing bikes throughout the neighborhood and, when we had allowance money, zooming toward the convenience store nearly two miles away, just at the end of Old Garners Ferry Road toward Hopkins. With no more than a few bucks between us to purchase stuffed brown paper bags of one-cent sweets like the candy-coated Big Bol gum and fruit-flavored taffy, packages of cheap duplex sandwich cookies, and chips, we raced down the bumpy road, its then-unlined pathway and significant narrowing making for tight two-way traffic.

Old Garners Ferry Road always seemed haunted, its dense woods adding to my unarticulated (to maintain my ten-year-old cool) but deeply felt fright. While the trees on a stretch of the road provided a bit of a canopy, a cooling respite from the sweltering Carolina summer, I felt as if something had been secreted away. Or as if something was lying in wait.

I am of course referring to vivid childhood fears of the unknown jumping out from the woods toward us vulnerable kids as we sped along, but reflecting now, too, on the known. Something, indeed, was there. Remained. As we crossed over the never smoothed-out bump announcing the tiny bridge over Mill Creek, we climbed the seemingly slight but arduous incline toward the store. Looking ahead, I would pedal as quickly as possible, the pastel-colored plastic tassels on the end of each handle flitting in the wind. I'd often rush toward the light offered by a clearing on the right-hand side. The awaiting brightness was made possible by the absence of trees in the front lawn of a home near the end of the road.

Roughly ten miles down the road behind our subdivision is the entrance to the Congaree National Park, which was designated as a US national monument in 1976 and established formally as a national park in 2003 in part to prevent further decimation from lumber companies' logging. Situated across twenty-six thousand acres in Hopkins, South Carolina, Congaree National Park contains the "largest intact expanse of old growth bottomland hardwood forest remaining in the southeastern United States" (Congaree National Park South Carolina). Home for thousands of years to indigenous peoples, the larger Congaree area is often mentioned as a significant site during the Revolutionary War. Both the British and the Patriots used it strategically as a campsite; it was the scene at which Francis "Swamp Fox" Marion ambushed British soldiers in 1781.

Congaree National Park is also home to visible remnants from the slavery era, including dikes and cattle mounds built by the hands of enslaved people in the lower portion of the Richland township to prevent roaming animals from drowning in high floodwaters. The enslaved workers often labored in the area, where they planted indigo, rice, cotton, corn, wheat, and oats in the alluvial bottomlands.

Today, Congaree National Park is home to dozens of champion trees, which receive such an esteemed designation because they are the largest of their species in the nation. The survival of bald cypress and tupelo trees across the centuries through weather events and logging is significant—as is the underrecognized fact that they are the sole living witnesses to the scene of nineteenth-century fugitive slave activity in the Congaree swamps.

* * *

Maroon communities were regular features of resistance across the Atlantic world. Variously named mocambos, quilombos, cimarron communities, palenqueros, and other site-specific designations, these isolated bands of fugitive, organized, and disciplined runaways, freepersons, and indigenous peoples were also unifying throughout the swamplands and backcountry of the southern United States beginning at least by the early eighteenth century.

The most famous US-based example is the case of the communities established in the Great Dismal Swamp of North Carolina and Virginia. While enslavers worried about recently disembarked saltwater Africans' propensity for confrontation and revolt as they came to grips with their fates, they soon realized that even those who were born into slavery and whose families had been in North America for generations often held no loyalty to their enslavers or to white-owned inanimate property. Captivity, certainly, was not natural. Neither was acquiescence.

Many sought covert and overt ways of subverting their bondage. A year before Denmark Vesey's infamous plan to take flight with thousands of slaves from Charleston to Haiti was thwarted and a decade before Nat Turner's bloody rebellion in Southampton County, Virginia, an enslaved man named Joe (alias Forest) made a fateful escape from his master, Mr. Carroll of Richland County, taking up residence in the swamps at the fork of the Wateree and Congaree Rivers in the lower portion of the district.

It is not known just how long Joe and his comrades had been on the run. They appear in the record soon after Joe and his fugitive cohort raided the plantation owned by George R. Ford on the Santee River in May 1821. The *Providence Gazette* explained about Joe in its July 18, 1821, coverage of the matter, "The subtle African continues his lodgement in the border of the swamps, and prowls around the neighbouring settlements, in defiance of all the efforts that have been made to apprehend him" (reprinted in Lockley 104). In the course of Ford and his men's attempt to fend off the rebels as they plundered his land, Ford was killed, prompting the obscene cataloging of and speculation about the death of this well-regarded attorney and planter in newspaper columns across the United States. Joe instantly became a most-wanted individual who would be subject to a relentless search, if only to salvage the now publicly fragile sense of southern white masculinity.

What I find most striking about Joe's case is the success of his vengeful reign and also the lengths to which the desperate white enslavers went to capture him and his band of men. An article in the June 6, 1821, issue of the *Boston Gazette* made transatlantic connections between Joe's fugitivity and that of a similarly shrewd outlaw from slavery in the Caribbean, referring to him as "an artful and bold fellow" who "approaches in hardihood to the character of 'Three Fingered Jack,' the celebrated bandit of Jamaica" (reprinted in Lockley 100). In the years that Joe eluded authorities, he traversed the South Carolina Midlands and ventured down into the Lowcountry and back again numerous times, leading groups of fugitives from slavery to freedom in newly forged communities in the swamplands.

In the interim, rumors of Joe sightings and tales about his supposed capture abounded, which had the effect of figuring South Carolina as a lawless laughingstock in the national media. Unable to negotiate the swamps with the prowess of the determined fugitives, white southern planters, militiamen, and volunteers were outwitted by the very beings whom they had deemed ignorant and mindless. In addition to encouraging plantation owners to be on guard for maroon raiders, lawmakers, journalists, and concerned white citizens issued caution to travelers along South Carolina roads. Ironically, the maroons had impeded the certainty of unrestricted white movement throughout the state.

In a trial of Jack, one of Joe's men who was captured during a close call for the entire maroon community, the jurors determined that Jack should be sentenced to execution by hanging, having been found guilty of being, at the very least, an accessory to the "unprovoked" crime of murder. Equally egregious, according to the media, was Jack's comportment during the trial. How dare a Negro, the sentiment of the time went, steal from a planter, torment white people across the state, and kill a white man without any remorse or outwardly expressed emotion. An unarticulated concern was the public airing out of the southern planter class who evidently could not control their human property, manage their investments, or protect their families. The *Charleston Courier* reported about Jack's unconcerned affect during the trial on June 4, 1821: "During the whole trial the prisoner exhibited no one mark of penitence or sorrow, but preserved the utmost stubbornness of features and of manner" (reprinted in Lockley 97).

With this eerie hint as to the psychology of the fugitive party and fears about similar forms of unrest in the future, white residents formed police groups and began offering incentives for their enslaved men to help with the manhunt. In 1823, Joe and a few other maroons were found and summarily killed. The militia dismembered Joe in what had become a southern rite for Negro combatants, particularly the masterminds: they placed Joe's head on a pole at the mouth of a creek. The prominent, gruesome spectacle served as a dire warning for those who held rebellious aspirations, though it did not have the long-lasting effect of eradicating fugitive flights.

The level of haunting that Joe and his compatriots were able to carry out and inspire on various plantations across a one-hundred-mile span through unsteady terrain and unpredictable weather conditions is fascinating. This armed pilfering of rations and acts of retribution occurred earlier than Frederick Douglass's impassioned call for fugitive resistance in his 1847 *Narrative of the Life of Frederick Douglass* and perhaps helped to inspire Douglass to take flight (along with other highly publicized acts of resistance). Douglass made the narrative decision to underscore the importance of strategically plotting to render enslavers unstable in their own sense of liberty via everyday forms of trickery, running away, and even eye-for-an-eye violence.

I still get goose bumps as Douglass's rhetoric hits fever pitch in his narrative. What a bold assertion to make in the nineteenth century, when a home in the North for a Black man was certainly no real protection. Sympathetic white northern readers were likely to be infuriated or take offense to Douglass spurring recalcitrance among the enslaved. Undaunted, Douglass offers a powerful catalog of the myriad injustices that he and others endured. His nonreligious antidote is a fitting countermeasure to evil:

> I would keep the merciless slaveholder profoundly ignorant of the means of flight adopted by the slave. I would leave him to imagine himself surrounded by myriads of invisible tormentors, ever ready to snatch from his infernal grasp his trembling prey. Let him be left to feel his way in the dark; let darkness commensurate with his crime hover over him; and let him feel that at every step he takes, in pursuit of the flying bondman, he is running the frightful risk of having his hot brains dashed out by an invisible agency. Let us render the tyrant no aid; let us not hold the light by which he can trace the footprints of our flying brother. (95)

In the two years after Joe's death, at least two other established maroon camps were discovered in South Carolina. The inhabitants were startled, but the majority of these flying fugitives were somehow able to avert capture, stealing away once more into seclusion.

***

In Lower Richland, one constantly navigates hallowed ground. The land had been reverently traversed and tended for millennia by indigenous peoples whose cultural ties to the region were stripped away in the service of placating European avarice. Untold, forgotten, and incomprehensible atrocities against the area's enslaved people occurred for generations, a cruel fate that ensured that wealthy Europeans and even their criminals, the theretofore ne'er-do-wells who were given a second chance via a ship's voyage to a new land, could make a life. Being *condemned to transportation*, or effectively banished from England to serve out prison sentences in the West Indies and North America via middle passages before 1776, was no doubt a grueling fate. But this was not an inheritable condition like enslavement. While they were not yet part of the propertied class, these mostly poor, uneducated laborers had a stake in the building and sustaining of a solid white-supremacist foundation in America. Their futures, the nation's future, would truly be made on the backs of enslaved Africans and their descendants. Each subsequent generation of African people in America would go on to experience the geography of containment anew, their access to mobility restricted by law and tradition, their movements policed and tracked at nearly every turn.

2

TRAIN

My elegant grandmother's death was decidedly inelegant. Grandma Isabell was a stoic, logical woman who fiercely loved her family, but her final years were marked by mental confusion and physical decline. Alzheimer's disease had addled her memories and rendered her child-like; it was necessary for others to tend to her every need.

I lamented that I had not taken time to speak with her more about her life and experiences years earlier, particularly regarding her travels and the short portion of her early adulthood spent in Philadelphia. My mom, aunts, and I always marvel at a lone photo that we have of Grandma in her young adult years. Her dark, generously applied lipstick causes us to giggle and wonder just *who* she was then. Before us. She was a child of Lower Richland farmers, born in the years just before the financial uncertainty of the Great Depression. In this photo of Grandma from the 1940s, perhaps taken in Philadelphia, she appears healthy and content. She is wearing a lovely dress and stylish hat, and she is adorned with jewelry. I'd never seen her so fancily attired.

The last time that I interacted with Grandma was devastating because she no longer knew who I was . . .

The author's grandmother Isabell. (Photo courtesy of the author)

who any of us were. She barely spoke to us family members who were visiting. But on that bright Carolina day, she liked me instantly and held my hand. She trusted me and smiled and followed my lead.

At her assisted living facility, Grandma was best friends with a white woman who, too, suffered a form of dementia, yet every day they roamed the building together and chatted, perhaps about the things they saw and felt. During our visit, my Aunt Hilda and I were somehow left in charge of the two of them for a bit, while the others spoke with the head nurse. In an effort to control their habit of wandering into spaces that were off limits, we suggested sitting in rocking chairs near a window and enjoying the view. They agreed, and we swayed and smiled at one another. Our motion prompted me to begin singing "My Bonnie Lies Over the Ocean," a song I learned while working as a receptionist at a similar facility during my undergraduate college years in North Charleston.

As I sang, a thick cry formed in my throat. The lyrics took on a new, urgent meaning, and the pleasant-to-sing tune itself dissolved into a mere feature. My tone went flat, but I controlled my voice as much as possible and continued.

> My Bonnie lies over the ocean
> My Bonnie lies over the sea
> My Bonnie lies over the ocean
> Oh, bring back my Bonnie to me . . .
>
> Bring back, bring back
> Oh, bring back my Bonnie to me, to me
> Bring back, bring back
> Oh, bring back my Bonnie to me.

We rocked, they hummed, and I sang. The words were affecting. Grandma was there but not. The rocking, our collective motion, pacified us as I sang of longed-for journeys and returns.

Shortly after that visit, Grandma suffered badly from a case of pneumonia and slipped away. While sorting through Grandma's papers, my mother and I came across a copy of my grandfather's death certificate. It was the first time that I had seen a record of someone's death, and I was unnerved. We remarked on the informal listing of his occupation as "Railroad Man" on an official document, deciding that that was probably Grandma's doing—an expression of her pride in her husband and his determination to take good care of his family. Besides the word choice, our sentiment was simply that official records of life and death—no matter the information they impart—tell us very little about the actual circumstances of someone's life or death.

In the 1990s, Aunt Hilda commissioned the renowned South Carolina artist Larry Lebby to create a portrait of my grandfather Thomas Gilford, the "Railroad Man," based on one of the few photographs of him that our family possessed. In the original black-and-white picture, my grandfather gazes expressionless, though not with disinterest, at the camera. He is wearing a hard hat for safety and a button-up work shirt. He is perhaps standing on the job site or at a stop on his way home. Like all of my known South Carolina ancestors before him, he was a laborer. He worked as a welder in steel plants and on railroads in Lower Richland in the mid-twentieth century. The railroad was just over a century old by then and part of the everyday existence for the area's residents, who saw its presence bring efficiency, new jobs, and gradual shifts in the area's social mores.

Larry Francis Lebby, *Steel Man*, 1992. (Gibbes Museum of Art, https://gibbesmuseum.pastperfectonline.com/webobject/1DA336B4-9145-4F43-B4CF-428698239626)

Recently, I discovered that a duplicate version of the india-ink portrait that Lebby created, which he had exhibited during his travels as far away as the Vatican, had been given the title "Steel Man" and sold to the Gibbes Museum in Charleston, South Carolina. For twenty years, my grandfather has stared directly back into the eyes of the museum's viewers, refashioned into a superman of sorts.

Here's something I know about the experience of my ancestors: exerting two centuries worth of generational labor on Lower Richland soil under the most brutal and corrupt circumstances must have involved herculean physical and mental strength.

The majority of my maternal line was enslaved near what became the town of Kingville, which was a site of an important train depot in the nineteenth century, particularly after its connection on the Southern Railroad Line was expanded in 1848. While Kingville boasted a reportedly decent hotel, a post office, stores, businesses, and homes, most of the town's white visitors did not appreciate its proximity to this portion of the Congaree River. In letters and journal entries, visitors referred to the town and its floodplain/swampland as "dismal" and as a "death hole." The potential for revelry at the end of daylong meetings or after a day's work on the railroad line was apparently minuscule in Kingville.

As I read these complaints, I wondered about whether and how my ancestors negotiated their bondage. Did any of them attempt to feel their way through the darkness and wade through what they viewed as *life-giving* rather than *dismal* swamps—or the train toward freedom and away from the state of living death that was enslavement? How did they survive? What other pathways and strategies did they use to get free?

***

The labor of enslaved and poor white people built and expanded South Carolina's railroad lines. Railroad companies and their attendant industries owned slaves as well as entered "hiring out" contracts with local plantation owners. A major sign of American progress and technological advancement,

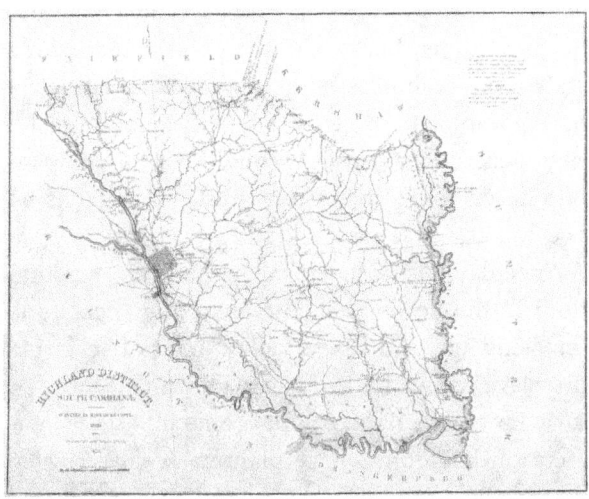

Mills's atlas of Richland County, South Carolina, in 1825. (Robert Mills, "Richland County," *Atlas of the State of South Carolina* [1825], accessed at http://digital.tcl.sc.edu/cdm/landingpage/collection/rma)

the presence of the railroad and increased interactions between southern and northern citizens must have given the sense that changes—wanted and unwanted—were afoot. The South Carolina Canal and Railroad Company (SCCRC) in what is now St. Matthews established its first completed track in 1833 to take advantage of the Industrial Revolution, which had a marked financial impact in the US North, with the railroad helping to propel the growth of the textile industry.

SCCRC soon found itself in a bind after white workers refused to deal with the risky nature of the job when the swamps became especially dangerous in the summer. Because of the pressing need for a stable set of laborers to dig roadbeds, to complete timberwork, and to perform repairs and other laborious tasks under any set of conditions, the company purchased some eighty-nine enslaved persons between 1845 and 1860.

Speculators developed substantial cotton plantations in the Lower Richland area, on which stood imposing homes that overlooked acres of fields and tiny slave cabins. In the early to mid-nineteenth century, Lower Richland County came into its own as a cotton kingdom whose planters' wealth rivaled that of their counterparts in the Lowcountry. The area's population remained fairly stagnant even into 1840, with the white population counted at 5,326, the enslaved community at 10,664, and free people of color at 407. (In 1860, the numbers inched up, but only slightly.) By 1842, southern railroads aided the area's financial success by transporting cotton more quickly than wagons and flatboats could—doing so, they created the hamlets of Gadsden, Kingville, and Hopkins Turnout.

The growth of the railroad in the South also compelled new and more creative forms of resistance among the enslaved. The railroad phenomenon gave more formalized terminology for the *technology* used by conductors of the Underground Railroad, a strategic network of safe houses and way stations that assisted tens of thousands of fugitive slaves in their travels toward free states, Canada, and Mexico beginning in the late eighteenth century.

I am utterly riveted by the trickster figure in early Black American stories about slavery and flight, as the cunning use of deception to actuate one's freedom is at once inspiring and sobering. The enslaved person's body had been marked as that which was possessed by and at the will of another. Imagine having the bravery to take control over such brutal, restrictive circumstances and even one's enslaved body—to assert temporary liberation and, sometimes, permanent escape from a master.

In 1848, William and Ellen Craft successfully ran away from slavery in Georgia by obtaining passes from their owners to travel freely for a few days around Christmas, utilizing the rare period of respite to carry out their fugitive flight via train. They dressed the fair-skinned Ellen in men's clothing and medical dressings, cut her hair, and added a pair of glasses to make her appear to be a disabled elderly white man traveling by train with his slave.

The Crafts' escape was an exercise of racial and gendered passing that secured their passage through the South to the northern United States and eventually to Liverpool, England, where they championed the abolitionist cause. Their subversive journeys by rail and ship presented moments at which the Crafts thought they would be found out as well as opportunities for Ellen to overhear white men's depraved musings about slavery and race. At one point during their fugitive passage, a slave trader on board with the Crafts mused to the captain about tamping down slave resistance: "If I was the President of this mighty United States of America, the greatest and freest country under the whole universe, I would never let no man, I don't care who he is, take a nigger into the North and bring him back here, filled to the brim, as he is sure to be, with d——d abolition vices, to taint all quiet niggers with the hellish spirit of running away" (Craft 26).

Beyond the captain's curious insistence that enslaved people would only get the notion that freedom was a possibility if they saw it in the North for themselves, the captain's staunch belief in American exceptionalism stands out here as an underrecognized feature of the antebellum era. To maintain order and control over human property in what proslavery citizens deemed to be an American utopia, several fugitive slave ordinances were written, including the most expansive, the Fugitive Slave Act of 1850.

Passed by the US Congress, the Fugitive Slave Act of 1850 amended the 1793 Act Respecting Fugitives from Justice, and Persons Escaping from the Service of Their Masters, at which several jurisdictions throughout various free states scoffed and passed their own laws to adjudicate the process and restrict the immediacy of the return of human property into slavery. The Fugitive Slave Act served as part of a compromise that would allow enslavers to capture slaves who escaped to free states and guide them on a passage back into slavery in the South without legal interference.

With the codification of fugitive laws on the horizon, the American reformer and abolitionist Samuel May penned a letter to the Crafts' host Dr. Estlin of Bristol, England, asking him to warn the Crafts that slave catchers were on their trail and that they would only be able to live truly liberated lives (undaunted by the threat of capture) if they fled to England:

> Shame, shame upon us, that Americans, whose fathers fought against Great Britain, in order to be FREE, should have to acknowledge this disgraceful fact! God gave us a fair and goodly heritage in this land, but man has cursed it with his devices and crimes against human souls and human rights. Is America the "land of the free, and the home of the brave?" God knows it is not; and we know it too. A brave young man and a virtuous young woman must fly the American shores, and seek, under the shadow of the British throne, the enjoyment of "life, liberty, and the pursuit of happiness." (Craft 56)

May's impassioned suggestion that the Crafts quit America was not at an overreaction. Bolstered by fugitive slave laws, deputized slave catchers were indeed on the hunt for the couple. Even the illegal importation of slaves, which had been abolished by US federal law in 1807 and by statute in South Carolina, was regularly practiced decades later. The nation's moral fiber, along with that of traders across the Atlantic world, was weak indeed. Slavery had been maintained via force, nonchalance by a stunning number of Americans, and moral hypocrisy. The very human impulse to protect oneself and one's kith and kin—in this case, the Crafts' assertion of their mobility—was enough to warrant severe punishment or death depending on the depravity of the owner.

* * *

During the Civil War, Kingville—one of the Lower Richland hamlets brought to life by the railroad—became a supply stop for the Confederate army until Union troops marched through the area, scorching Columbia and much of the surrounding area in 1865. General Edward E. Potter and his troops destroyed Kingville's hotel, depots, agent's house, the Congaree River Bridge, and three thousand feet of railroad track. In the postbellum period, my poor but industrious formerly enslaved family members worked to rebuild the town or moved nearby. The Kingville archive (compromised, like most archives of historical Black life in the United States are) tells a story about place and escape, intersecting histories and desires. It was a bustling town, with the rail whistle singing vibrantly in the background, but yet still a town with something dismal restricting its heart.

Scant traces of Kingville proper exist. I am aware of two markers: one that merely states the name of the place/train stop alongside a railroad track and another at a post office in Hopkins. My mother and her siblings often speak about Kingville fondly, though they were born long after the town became a ghost. They do not recall many exact stories imparted to them about the place, yet a feeling of pride about that historic town and its Black community remains. It was one of the pieces of history about which they remember their grandparents and people of that generation marveling.

In the immediate aftermath of the Civil War, however, most formerly enslaved people in the Lower Richland area signed labor contracts with their former owners. It was probably the easiest short-term solution for the newly freed population because they knew the land like their own heartbeats and they had few other prospects. Staying in place amid the new order of things came with the assurance of building community with known folks, so, for some time at least, they remained.

I first confirmed the names of my grandmother's great-grandparents, who were born in the 1840s, in an 1866 labor contract filed away and later digitized in the Freedmen's Bureau's archives for South Carolina. As I sat in a Harlem cafe on a Saturday afternoon, the pieces suddenly fell into place. I sat startled for a moment and then looked around at chatty friend groups and busy college students, as if anyone knew or cared about what I had found. I wanted to tell someone the good news, but I knew no one there. I was far from home.

Refocusing, I again carefully assembled and correlated all of my pieces of solid evidence, including slave schedules from 1850 and 1860, a local genealogist's separately prepared records about the community, death certificates from the early twentieth century, and decades of census records that linked the people represented in all of these documents.

I gulped and, surprising myself, began to silently cry. Here was confirmation of some things I knew or had surmised about my family's enslavement and their working-class existence, their labor in the fields of Lower Richland. I was overwhelmed and sad and angry about centuries of *a past* that I clearly had not even experienced firsthand. It was my legacy. My ancestral generations had lived hard, hard lives. As I made connections about the truth of their lives (and combined with some speculations about how they might have been affected by myriad laws, events, and societal trends), I fell in love with these people immediately. Their names alone had removed some of the abstractness of knowing that *my kin* had been enslaved. Now, I could place their history more accurately.

I touched one of the digitized "Xs" on my laptop screen. That single-letter marking had been made in the unsteady hand of my third great-grandfather Louis (listed as "Lewis" in the record). This was his agreement that he, his wife Letty, and their family member Binkey would provide the executor of their former owner Wright Denley's estate "a portion of the crop," which for their small household required "two bales of cotton and fifteen bushels of corn" each year in exchange for their use of the living quarters, firewood, and the land and equipment to farm on the Greenfield Plantation. In pounds, they had agreed to produce an astounding 960 pounds of cotton and 840 pounds of corn for Denley's estate.

The conducting of genealogical quests is a kind of traveling resistance, a temporal exercise in which one can retrieve long-buried, if sorrowful, histories. Just as the presence of the railroad transported travelers to more desired locations and expanded the ways that free and enslaved early African Americans could imagine the possibilities for their future mobility, the tracks and rails of genealogy greatly impact the ways that the family details unearthed confirm (track), belie (throw long-held beliefs off the rails), and add to (move forward) one's understanding of the past and present.

Genealogy can also be addicting, maddening, confusing, and exhilarating. I still know very little about my third great-grandparents and virtually nothing about their parents or their parents' parents. But I continue to work to arrange the pieces. The things we learn about our family members' painful deaths, infidelities, arduous journeys, bad decisions, and heartbreaking life circumstances can take the breath away. Take my breath away. I find myself wondering about my ancestors' dreams deferred, their joyous experiences *anyhow*, and details of the reminiscing and turns of phrase that made them crack up with good ol' belly laughter.

Engaging in genealogical quests sometimes means that narratives that we think we know about familial connections and the historical order of things will be proven incorrect or incomplete. It is certainly not required, but I feel as though I must face this challenge. My desire to address this feeling of dispossession as well as my eagerness to know is part of my inheritance. I am most concerned with the ways that my ancestors' lives and experiences might give me a clearer view into my own life and those of others who were reared in or are descendants of the people who have lived parallel and unequal existences in Lower Richland over nearly three centuries.

In what will certainly be a shock to my family, I have often felt a desire for the formerly enslaved to make themselves evident. I am not asking for a seance or a dance with the devil or anything of the sort. An ancestor guiding my journey toward a rare find in an archive will do.

***

> I wish every vessel that would go to Africa
> to bring slaves here—could sink before they
> reached her soil. I would give up every [cent]
> I own on earth if I could stop the slave trade.
> (Brevard 44)

As a war between the states became likely, the Hopkins, South Carolina–based enslaver and cautious investor in railroad companies Keziah Goodwyn

Hopkins Brevard kept a diary to work through her anxiety about the increasing likelihood of Northern aggression. Written between July 22, 1860, and April 15, 1861, Brevard's diary largely captures the mundane aspects of her typical day: she canned vegetables and cooked a good bit with her trusted enslaved laborers, transacted business, and hosted and visited with her friends and loved ones. In my attempts to grasp more about my family's history in Lower Richland, one person I have learned a great deal about is her.

Brevard was a rarity in Lower Richland in that she thrived in the patriarchal world of slaveholding. She seemed to chart her own course, a woman who pleaded often to God but admitted that she was not terribly religious, as most of her counterparts claimed to be. She was a member of, and paid her tithes to, Beulah Baptist Church, visiting for service infrequently. The fifty-seven-year-old widow, who was propertied via her father's bequests and her own financial acumen, owned at least three plantations, two hundred slaves across Lower Richland, a grist mill, and a fair share of railroad stock whose steady performance, ironically, probably triggered Brevard's worry about the quickness with which change was happening in the South.

In many of the twentieth-century historical engagements with Brevard's life, she is lauded for her economic success and figured as a woman of her time who is held in awe for all she was able to achieve. Brevard's diary is filled with iterations of "Lord save our country," especially as she descended into a kind of madness and state of paranoia not only about the possibility of Abraham Lincoln's election to the presidency and the threat of a pending war but also about her fears that her slaves, whom she referred to as a "multitude of half barbarians," despised her, stole from her, and might do her harm. Throughout the diary, Brevard expresses particular disgust with the enslaved women on her plantations, noting that they were sexually promiscuous and cunning. In her reflections on the morality of slavery, Brevard writes that white enslavers had saved the primitive Africans from themselves with religious and moral instruction and that she would gladly send them back to Africa now that their presence had caused such unrest in the nation.

Their presence—as if enslaved people and their families had elected to live imperiled lives in a foreign land. Brevard goes on to complain in a hypocritical moment of projection whose level of irrationality would be humorous if it did not involve a topic as horrific as the institution of slavery, "A degraded population is a curse to a country. Negroes are as deceitful & lying as any people can well be—Lord give me better feelings towards them. (Forgive me Lord, for unkind thoughts & have mercy on me!)" (42). It is telling that Brevard's parenthetical messages to her Lord convinced some twentieth-century historians that she was really rethinking her racist beliefs. In fact, she detested that the men in some white families had lain sexually with Black women, not because of the assaults or coercion involved but because white men desired them and had children with beings that she considered innately inferior and immoral, willing participants. Brevard found unnerving the idea of white and Black people might choose to commingle consensually in a democratic future without a racial hierarchy in place.

Throughout her diary, Brevard often recorded the disturbing nightmares she had of fire and violence. These night terrors were probably prompted by her waking-hour fears of retribution from the enslaved community. According to Brevard's angry entries, many of her slaves *deigned* to talk back to her and worked slowly just to spite her. Brevard was convinced that they and other enslaved people in Lower Richland were far more cunning and intelligent than they let on.

She also was worried about the potential devastation that the Union soldiers' arrival in South Carolina would bring. While Brevard endured heartbreak and the usual stressors of family and business, her entire life had been one characterized by rare economic privilege. The threat of losing it all animated her diary entries, with her frantic, repetitive expressions suggesting a descent into paranoia. The prospect of a dramatic, devastating shift in her livelihood was too much. On December 10, 1860, Brevard wrote,

> This is a blustering day. I am really uneasy about fire, I must send & hear from sister—poor sister,

but perhaps you are as happy as I am, all comforts are from God & he blesses his own as they deserve. I hope & trust in God as soon as Secession is carried out—we of the South begin to find a way to get all the Negroes sent back to Africa & let the generations to come after us live in more peace than we do—I can't see how we are ever to be safe with them in our midst—I wish every soul of them were in Africa contented in their own homes—let us begin on corn bread & live in peace & security—as long as they are here & number so many more than the whites there is no safety any way—Men of the South—I fear our end is near & the [Yankees] will glory over their work. I do hate a Northern Abolitionist—Lord forgive me—but who can love those whose highest ambition is to cut our throats. (58)

Some historians have written about Brevard with a level of awe and admiration that escapes me. Her desire to cast these Lower Richland ancestors out—to send them back *after* they have created her unearned wealth—is a brutal irony. I feel no affinity toward Brevard as a woman, and I refuse to extend a tinge of generosity for her emotional reaction to her self-created circumstances.

Because, of course, despite Brevard's requests for forgiveness, which immediately follow her negative thoughts about Black people, she refused to give up slaveholding and her diversified financial investments.

Brevard certainly did not offer recompense to those who continued to labor on her properties in the aftermath of slavery. The country's land, laws, and all therein was the property of white people, in her estimation. Brevard rationalized her commitment to the institution and the southern agricultural order of her day thusly: "Would I not be better in heart if I had no slaves? This is hard to answer—God has given them to us" (February 1, 1861, 85). A gift from God: that is how she imagined the forced movement toward, and Black confinement within, the life of slavery.

* * *

In my teens, I was a member of the youth and mass choirs at New Light Beulah Baptist Church in Hopkins. One year, New Light Beulah and Beulah Baptist attempted to revive an old tradition of gathering during Thanksgiving in a kind of demonstration of Christian brotherhood. The two churches had a profound, interconnected history. Beulah Baptist Church, Brevard's rarely visited congregation, was founded in 1805, and the sanctuary served as the worship place for the white and enslaved communities on alternate Sundays and for a short period in the postbellum era.

I imagine that because they shared a church building, the white congregants felt as if they held to a kinder, more benevolent form of slavery. Brevard certainly suggested throughout her diary that although she was unceasingly generous and caring to her slaves, they were only concerned about themselves, rarely listened to her, and treated her with the utmost disdain. She allowed them to attend Beulah dismissively, remarking on what she viewed as their peculiar tradition of taking communion on the fifth Sunday in March 1861, as if they had a choice in when and how they had access to the church.

The postbellum period resulted in new racial relations in the area and across the South. After a couple of years of tense and sometimes violent arguments over who truly owned the church building, the Black Beulah Baptist congregants eventually established themselves separately as New Light Beulah Baptist Church, meeting outside in a clearing until they could build their own place of worship. The final straw in the struggle over the church property ownership had come in 1871 when the white church member Jesse Reese Adams opted to move his family into the Beulah Baptist sanctuary, lying in wait, so to speak, for the Black congregants to arrive. The unsuspecting congregants were met by the determined Adams and his weapon and were forced to leave the site. They realized that they would have to create their own sanctuary. No peace would be found there.

Just before the Thanksgiving season in the 1990s, a member of the mass choir began fussing, to no one in particular in the alto section, about the expectation that we would attend the program at Beulah Baptist: "It don't make no sense. I don't want to go over there." This was a program for which Beulah's own choir members, we would discover just before the event started, refused to perform, as they confessed to being too embarrassed by their lack of talent. It was another instance, the choir member muttered, of Black folks having to go along with what white folks wanted. Would our righteous presence signal something akin to forgiveness for centuries of dispossession, poverty, and discrimination? Did they think the invitation served as some sort of apology or reparation, given that both congregations would now sit and worship together?

Less concerned by our choir's call as a ministry, the angry choir member (and others, like myself, who nodded or "m-hmed" in agreement) could not simply abide the racial optics of the event without comment. While we attended that year's Thanksgiving program and sang as our choir director had promised we would, I will never forget the choir member's angrily articulated promise to never go back to Beulah Baptist. She and her family shared a surname and perhaps bloodlines with some of Beulah Baptist's founders and their descendants, but they were not truly kin. The past was too present. *We had not been given to them.*

I am not certain what songs we performed at that fall program, but one of my favorite hymns, "We're Marching to Zion," is a possibility. The message of movement toward eventual triumph in the third stanza, especially the aspect that I read now as having a subversive double meaning regarding new world-making, strikes me as the most powerful element.

> Let those refuse to sing,
> who never knew our God;
> but children of the heavenly King,
> but children of the heavenly King
> may speak their joys abroad,
> may speak their joys abroad.
> We're marching to Zion,
> beautiful, beautiful Zion.
> We're marching upward to Zion;
> the beautiful city of God.

* * *

Sometime in the early 1980s, Grandma Isabell and I paid a visit to the St. Phillip AME Church cemetery in Eastover. We were visiting the graves of family members from the Gilford side, including those belonging to my grandfather and long-ago-deceased members of his family.

To say that I was frightened is an understatement. Grandma was known to have dreams that came true, giving my siblings, cousins, and me the sense of the existence of other worlds—and an eerie feeling that we're not alone in this world. Though Grandma was a Holiness preacher, her spirituality, gifts, and abilities seemed to transcend.

On that particular day, we walked toward the far reaches of the cemetery. The graves extended quite a ways back into the distance and, of course, time. As we moved from grave to grave, Grandma sometimes speaking to or about the dead, I noticed that one headstone differed from the others because of its height and detail, which caught my attention. I pointed at the headstone to draw Grandma's attention to it, and she quickly admonished me in a hushed voice to never, ever to point at a grave, lest something negative would befall me.

I wondered but did not ask, Who would hear or see me? What would they do to me? I remain intrigued by ghostly matters in the aftermath of slavery and the ways that the enslaved may have wanted to be remembered, their names articulated in recognition and reverence much like the embodied ghost-child desires in Toni Morrison's *Beloved* when she utters the plaintive, "there is no one to want me to say me my name." What can the unearthing of our enslaved ancestors' pasts reveal to us about our present? Our futures?

The work of uncovering lost and intentionally buried histories about slavery is daunting but necessary. Historians, writers, and artists who attempt to craft thorough narratives about slavery from archival sources often find themselves carrying out what Saidiya Hartman refers to as *critical fabulation*, the stitching together of related (but not necessarily immediately connected) pieces with informed speculation to contend with the archive's stubborn gaps. During an interview with Thora Siemsen about aesthetics and archives of slavery, Hartman aptly suggests that narrative itself might be the only possible "redress for the monumental crime that was the transatlantic slave trade." Her account is gripping: "One of the things I think is true, which is a way of thinking about the afterlife of slavery in regard to how we inhabit historical time, is the sense of temporal entanglement, where the past, the present and the future, are not discrete and cut off from one another, but rather that we live the simultaneity of that entanglement. This is almost common sense for black folk. How does one narrate that?" (Siemsen). Archival fissures paired with the circuitness of time render engagements with slavery and its afterlife uneasy and entangled indeed: how does one write it while in it?

***

In my recent travels to the Congaree National Park, the rangers have made mention of its historic maroon community, the existence of cattle mounds, and other evidence of Black life in the swamplands, in response to my presence there as a researcher. When I have inquired about the possibility of conducting a small expedition on my own, I have been advised that while solo explorations of the park are indeed possible, many of the areas would be too difficult to traverse. I would need to dress properly, covering my legs and arms. Good hiking shoes were suggested as well as the knowledge that some of the area would require navigation by watercraft. I would have to fight off mosquitoes and other nagging, biting insects and a range of wild animals, and I would have to deal with miles of unsteady footing in the suffocating heat. It would be uncomfortable but relatively safe on established pathways, I was assured. Yet the truth was that what I desired to see—evidence of Joe's maroon community and other settlements—were unmarked and impossible to visit with surety due to the overgrowth and the lack of signposts that mark these sites in sustainable ways since they were last found.

These conditions were not tenable, but I perked up as a park ranger told me about the vocal spirits in that area of the Congaree. Over the years, other park staff members have corroborated and added to their scripts a haunting tale found in the physician and lay ethnographer Dr. Edward C. L. Adams's supremely problematic and racistly framed, yet invaluable collections of tall tales, myths, and Black cultural scenes from the Lower Richland area of the Congaree.

Adams, a descendant of one of Lower Richland's wealthy slaveholding families, determined that there was a "primitive" quality to the African-descended people in the area, not unlike what he deemed to be the uniqueness of the Gullah community in the Lowcountry. He writes in the prologue to his 1928 volume *Nigger to Nigger*, "It is remarkable that so definite a survival of the negro of Africa as modified by white relationships should be maintained in such purity in the very midst of so exclusive a white culture" (Adams 109).

As a purported insider, Adams put on his ethnographer's hat and became a participant-observer of the laborers who worked on his land and of other Black people in Lower Richland. He assures the reader that he was friendly with members of the community, some of whom were technically his relatives via slavery-era abuses and that he was allowed in on certain aspects of Black Lower Richland culture, though the extent to which his informants might be pulling his leg, leaving out true group knowledge and private feelings about race and the social order during the dangerous Jim Crow era, or otherwise subverting Adams's gaze is unknown.

According to the myth shared with Adams by his witty interlocutors in *Congaree Sketches*, a Lower Richland slave trader named Old Man Rogan was infamous for taking pleasure in separating enslaved loved ones from each other, husband from wife, mother from child. When he was not working, Old Man Rogan's favorite pastime was fishing in an area called Boggy Gut in Beaufort County. Since Old Man Rogan's death, explained the storyteller, his evil "sperrit . . . ain't got no res'" (Adams 48).

At the time that Adams collected these tales, locals apparently reported seeing chained enslaved men bent over with their heads in their hands in defeat at Boggy Gut. They heard the devastating cries of babies, mothers calling for their children, followed by the sound of Old Man Rogan, whose spirit was restless and unsettled, laughing at the misery that he has caused by separating kith and kin and creating generational breaches that would last in perpetuity. The dissonance produced by the distress and irreverent mocking is said to travel from the Lowcountry and across bodies of water, including reverberations at the Congaree in Lower Richland.

Because I have observed slavery's aftereffects in Lower Richland and throughout South Carolina in the sometimes surface-level ways that we South Carolinians interact with each other across class and race, the memorialization of Confederates and the ensuing debates over the past few decades, and the obvious changes in landscape and wealth as one literally crosses railroad tracks, the persistence of such articulations of pain heartens me. I have not heard or seen insistent, ancient traces like those in Old Man Rogan's tale for myself, but recurring reports of their sonic immanence offer some sense that the victims of such tragedies will not allow their stories to be forgotten. These narratives—oral, written, mythic, and speculative—will have to suffice. They travel toward us by their own means.

* * *

As Brevard feared would happen, South Carolina's infrastructure suffered badly during the Civil War. Somehow her property was spared the extensive destruction seen in other areas of Lower Richland and the state of South Carolina. As the Union army made its way toward Lower Richland, hundreds of

Richard Taylor, "Kingville Depot in Lower Richland County." (The State Media Company [Columbia, SC], November 4, 1958, https://cdm16817.contentdm.oclc.org/digital/collection/p16817coll21/id/1409)

enslaved men from Lower Richland plantations were assigned to dangerous work details in the battlefields, where they were forced to work for Confederate troops on the sea islands or sent to refugee camps set up at the Kingville depot and elsewhere. Brevard had only her misgivings about the new racial order with which to contend.

In the Lowcountry at the Combahee River, Harriet Tubman, one of the great, fearless conductors of the Underground Railroad—who famously reasoned, "there was one of two things I had a right to: liberty or death; if I could not have one, I would have the other"—worked with the Union army to usher scores of enslaved people from the South Carolina coast to contraband camps. The war lent the Underground Railroad the possibility for an increase in the number of travelers.

For those who remained in Lower Richland, tenant farming and sharecropping, indeed, became the order of the day, and the region returned to cotton cultivation. Prompted by financial exigencies as well as the Freedmen's Bureau, which addressed the concerns about enslaved people's access to work, education, health, and overall well-being, Brevard and her contemporaries entered into legal, yet unethical, labor contracts with members of their formerly enslaved communities that tied many of them to the land for generations.

One of the most significant and promising features of the Reconstruction era in South Carolina is that the state government attempted to redistribute land in a way that would offer a pathway to ownership: the new owners would work the land to pay off the debt for their allotted parcel over time. The South Carolina Land Commission was the brainchild of the more than three hundred Black Republicans who held office in South Carolina during Reconstruction (around 130 of them had been enslaved).

South Carolina's Republicans worked to offer government social services and protections from white domestic terrorism to the newly freed community, ensuring that they had the opportunity to establish themselves in this new society. Republican initiatives would endow some landless Black people and poor white people with an opportunity to build better lives for themselves and their families, but those hopeful days would not last long.

When the Democrats assumed power in 1876, they quickly shuttered the Land Commission and worked to limit African Americans' freedom as promised by the Reconstruction Amendments to the US Constitution. South Carolina became a hotbed of domestic terrorism, with organizations like the Ku Klux Klan and the Red Shirts leading voter-intimidation activities and lynching campaigns there and across the South. Working oftentimes in concert with these lawless, murderous bands, southern lawmakers strategized to reconstruct white supremacy in the South by further codifying their hatred into the law.

***

Jacob Stroyer's 1879 memoir *My Life in the South* chronicles aspects of his experiences on the land that eventually became Kensington Plantation in Eastover. Writing as a formerly enslaved person turned AME preacher based in Massachusetts, Stroyer ruminates throughout the narrative on the relations between master and slave, the peculiar role of Black slave drivers, episodes of murderous violence carried out by a depraved slave catcher, and instances of slave fugitivity in the South.

Stroyer's vignettes are harrowing. Though he does not articulate anything directly about his want of familial reunification, the postslavery publication of the text serves as a subtle warning about his contemporary moment that also offered him space for a kind of public purging or possibly even cathartic release, though he does not detail his anger or emotional pain in the published record. Stroyer knew, however, that his experiences were not unique in their horror; the inhumanity enacted by Lower Richland's enslavers and their hired help, however, was unconscionable. What did one do with the burden of various slavery-related traumas, particularly as they were triggered by the uncertainties of Reconstruction and domestic terrorism at the end of the nineteenth century?

A tragic scene punctuates Stroyer's narrative. He recounts the response of his former enslaver, Richard Singleton, to his near financial ruin in the 1850s. To stem bankruptcy, Singleton selected a large portion of his enslaved population with whom he would part and sell in Louisiana. This unfortunate group included Stroyer's sisters and other loved ones.

These sold people traveled by train. Stroyer describes the devastating moment just before Singleton's slaves departed the station:

> Imagine a mass of uneducated people shedding tears and yelling at the tops of their voices in anguish and grief.

The victims were to take the cars from a station called Clarkson turnout, which was about four miles from master's place. The excitement was so great that the overseer and driver could not control the relatives and friends of those that were going away, as a large crowd of both old and young went down to the depot to see them off. Louisiana was considered by the slaves as a place of slaughter, so those who were going did not expect to see their friends again. While passing along, many of the negroes left their masters' fields and joined us as we marched to the cars; some were yelling and wringing their hands while others were singing little hymns that they were accustomed to for the consolation of those that were going away. . . .

While the cars were at the depot, a large crowd of white people gathered, and were laughing and talking about the prospect of negro traffic; but when the cars began to start and the conductor cried out, "all who are going on this train must get on board without delay," the colored people cried out with one voice as though the heavens and earth were coming together, and it was so pitiful, that those hard hearted white men who had been accustomed to driving slaves all their lives, shed tears like children. As the cars moved away we heard the weeping and wailing from the slaves, as far as human voice could be heard; and from that time to the present I have neither seen nor heard from my two sisters, nor any of those who left Clarkson depot on that memorable day. (42–44)

Observing from the relative safety of New England, Stroyer insists on the humanity of the enslaved. Though the prominent white men who attest to his religious fidelity and good character in the book's front matter state that the narrative is a historical study of a time that has fortunately passed, Stroyer actually offers a subversive critique of the nation's political and social inequities as well as the unchecked violence of the so-called New South. At the same time that the railway offered access and mobility and signaled progress, it also served as a mode of transport that actuated the spiriting of human beings away from their kin and loved ones in the name of capitalism.

The postbellum forms of neoslavery and open articulations of violently racist sentiment compelled Stroyer to bear witness to the time of slavery and its unfortunate aftermath. He concludes his narrative with a nod to the presentness of slavery and the repulsive philosophies that rationalized its necessity and legality: "[Slavery] has made a lasting impression upon my mind. But however lasting, I make no complaint against those who held me in slavery. My war is upon ignorance, which has been and is the curse of my race" (83). The descendants of Lower Richland's enslaved community would go on to contend with Black codes and Jim Crow laws that limited their access to public accommodations, holding onto the possibilities of gaining a truer sense of liberty in America via migratory flights and fervent attempts at financial upward mobility.

3

AUTOMOBILE

The slave went free; stood a brief moment in the sun; then moved back again toward slavery.
—W. E. B. Du Bois, *Black Reconstruction in America*

Someday you be walking down the road and you hear something or see something going on. So clear. And you think it's you thinking it up. A thought picture. But no. It's when you bump into a rememory that belongs to somebody else. . . . If you go there—you who never was there—if you go there and stand in the place where it was, it will happen again; it will be there for you, waiting for you. . . . Nothing ever dies.
—Toni Morrison, *Beloved*

As I stand in Eastover, South Carolina, on the side of the road beside the closed and locked gate to the Wavering Place Plantation, I recall Morrison's words from *Beloved* about slavery's continuations—the haunting of slavery. Today's air is humid and heavy, and the sun's rays are relentless, exacerbated by my deep longing to know, to feel some measure of the momentousness of that time and its aftermath into the twentieth century.

The news of liberation no doubt stunned the enslaved community in Lower Richland and those throughout the South. I imagine that these newly freed individuals expressed sheer awe at the notion, coupled with immediate anxiety about how they would take care of themselves as well as their loved ones. Perhaps they hugged one another and smiled, then gathered together in a clearing to discuss what all of it meant.

Should they flee immediately to the city, where they probably had never traveled, for a chance at life? Or migrate toward other states in search of lost family members? How would they get there, and with what and whom would they travel? How did notions of community begin to shift in such a moment? Did fear overwhelm them?

Was there a grandmother who whispered calmly to those who were afraid, much like the spirit of *Beloved*'s formerly enslaved Baby Suggs had when she encouraged her granddaughter Denver, who was afraid to leave her family home in Ohio during the Reconstruction era? Denver was so frightened by the agonizing stories that had been imparted to her, the slavery-related traumas that had taken their toll on her family, and the prospect of encountering the evilest of the white community who "prowl at will":

> Denver stood on the porch in the sun and couldn't leave it. Her throat itched; her heart kicked—and then Baby Suggs laughed, clear as anything.

BABY SUGGS: You mean I never told you nothing about Carolina? About your daddy? You don't remember nothing about how come I walk the way I do, and about your mother's feet, not to speak of her back? I never told you all that? Is that why you can't walk down the steps? My Jesus my.

DENVER: But you said there was no defense.

BABY SUGGS: There ain't.

DENVER: Then what do I do?

BABY SUGGS: Know it, and go on out the yard. Go on. (288)

Though there were some highlights to the project of Reconstruction in South Carolina, the truth of the matter is that the positive aspects—liberation, political representation, and the franchise—were short-lived, curbed by a white southern desire to return society back to its supremacist roots. The glimmers of Black people's mobility, intellect, and enterprise in the late nineteenth century, so soon after their bondage, startled and infuriated white southerners. Licking their wounds, they strove, often violently, to redeem their severe wartime losses. They wanted us constrained again.

All of my maternal great-grandparents were the children and grandchildren of these emancipated people. They were born in Lower Richland in the late 1890s, and the details of their desires to leave for other locales remain unknown to me. The South, of course, was no easy geography with which to contend. Its white population's general disdain for Black people and their cultural ways was evinced by cruel barrages, particularly on those who seemed to step *out of their places* by achieving notable levels of upward mobility. To imagine the experience of living in the early years of the Black twentieth century means always to revisit the more distant past.

I often contemplate newly freed Black people's outlooks regarding raising their children. How did they live, or parent, with the knowledge that white terrorists were in their midst, determined to intimidate and keep Black folks marginalized? When one does not have much power—social, political, or otherwise—silence can take on a debilitating function in the domestic space. Articulated fears, too, make impressions on children, increasing their propensity for timidity and anxiety about the future. How do you talk to your Black children about hope, imagining something better, or burning it all down and creating worlds anew? These are enduring questions. For though the white supremacists' "reasons" for surveilling and threatening Black people in the twentieth century were often steeped in old stereotypes about Black people's supposed laziness and aggression, nothing seemed to worry those projecting, vicious degenerates more than African American progress.

* * *

The Great Migration began in earnest in the 1910s with the exodus of some 1.6 million African Americans from the South to the US Northeast and Midwest. Economic uncertainty, the lack of jobs, restrictive societies, and the boll weevil's destruction of cotton fields throughout the South compelled movement to potentially better lives elsewhere.

With the continued movements of African Americans through permanent migrations during that first and then the much larger second wave of the Great Migration into the mid-twentieth century, which saw the exodus of an additional five million African Americans from the US South to the North, Midwest, and West, came significant limitations on their movements that threatened the seeming egalitarianism of the American landscape in the 1950s–1960s. White southern lawmakers and citizens bristled at efforts to recruit African Americans to northern cities, even passing legislation to make it illegal for agents to solicit Black southern labor. Despite these laws, African Americans like my grandfather attempted to negotiate and/or escape suffocating southern landscapes in the early to mid-twentieth century, drawing on their own maps, their own ways of knowing about the world.

Perhaps the most famous of the formal compendiums of Black navigational tools in that era was *The Negro Motorist Green Book*, which offered travel and safety advice to African American travelers who were planning to proceed by car through sundown towns to their destinations, providing lists of hotels,

Cover of the 1956 issue of *The Negro Travelers' Green Book*. (Victor H. Green, *The Negro Travelers' Green Book* [New York: Victor H. Green, 1956], USC South Caroliniana Library, Columbia, http://library.sc.edu/digital/collections/greenbook.html)

private homes, and businesses willing to welcome these travelers during the height of segregation and racial strife. *The Green Book* functioned as a kind of alternative road map to help render travel a more secure and feasible prospect for its readers.

Unbound and undeterred, my family members—mostly my great-aunts and great-uncles in their youth—along with other African Americans, determinedly asserted their mobility through various means in hopes of triumphing over the burden of racism. Though it must have been unnerving and remarkably lonely to strike out this way into the unknown, some of my migrating family members went on to earn well-paying jobs in Detroit, Philadelphia, and New York, before retiring back home in the South in the 1970s and 1980s.

The Green Book was not the only vital travel resource. Renowned for its attractive covers that featured graphics often printed in boldly saturated hues, *Holiday* magazine published compelling features on travel to domestic and international locales for a largely white American readership and, most significantly for this discussion, contained essays on contemporary issues within and outside American society from 1946 to 1977, when the magazine was sold and became *Travel* magazine.

Armed with a copy of *Travelguide*, which like *The Green Book* assisted Black motorists in their quest to travel the American road as safely as possible to their destinations, the author John A. Williams ventured on the American road on a *Holiday* magazine assignment to "take the pulse of the country" without, his editors implored, focusing too much on the question of civil rights. Their insistence on such an exercise of emotional restraint and writerly deceit ultimately

Cover of the 1955 issue of *Travelguide*. (Schomburg Center for Research in Black Culture, Jean Blackwell Hutson Research and Reference Division, The New York Public Library; "Travelguide 1955," New York Public Library Digital Collections, http://digitalcollections.nypl.org/items/6072f8d0-78f8-0137-075d-0b584be463b4)

demonstrated the limitations of *Holiday* magazine's progressive vision as well as revealed Williams's initial Black bourgeois outlook, which transforms as he realizes the uncertainty of his privilege and mobility (Williams vii).

In a telling moment after Williams has gladly left his journey throughout the racist, segregated South and has entered what he thinks is a more welcoming "zenith of normality" in Chicago, he accepts an invitation to participate on a local radio show to discuss his writing career and the civil rights struggle. Williams is stunned by a caller who emphatically tells him to go back to Africa (Williams 85).

Unnerved, Williams later gets back on the road and reflects the psychic escape afforded by his automobility: "I let the car out and it jumped ahead, moving cleanly and easily, and the joy of having so much power at toe tip filled me completely. . . . There had been times in the South when I hated to leave the car because it formed a vault of safety. But in New England and when I was emerging from the South, I did not want to get out of the car because of the sense of power it gave me; power to move rapidly, for miles, at so little cost of energy to myself" (Williams 86–87).

The feeling that Williams describes is the thrill of liberation. His passionate reaction is a sign that marketing and industry efforts to compel such an affective response to the possession and control of an automobile were indeed effective. The automobile industry was big business, as it was, by the mid-twentieth century, inextricably bound up with notions of the American Dream. The Ford Motor Company had perfected the assembly line technique and went on to manufacture more than fifteen million Model T cars between 1913 and 1927. In 1950, eight million automobiles of all makes and models were produced in the United States, and by 1958, sixty-seven million cars were registered.

The 1956 Interstate Highway Act led to the creation more that ninety-two thousand miles of highway across the nation with multiple and wider lanes, and much of American culture made references to road travel, from commercial advertising and music to the popularity of drive-in movies and restaurants. Major technological advances in automobile production convincingly suggested that the nation was entering another era of modernity in which the everyday person could be afforded the opportunity to travel on their own schedule and in relative privacy, with total power over their mobility.

* * *

In *I Wonder as I Wander*, the writer Langston Hughes includes reflections on his travels through the US South in the 1930s for a poetry tour accompanied by the artist Zell Ingram. On this leg of their travels (the pair had also traveled extensively in the Caribbean), Hughes and Ingram packed a car with their personal items and books for sale. Their passages in the region gives a series of glimpses into the kinds of mobility that the new widespread access to automobiles offered and also to the kinds they did not.

Often, Black social networks were just as vital for travel success as the infrastructures—the cars, the roads—on which mobility seemed to take place. For instance, the great educator, philanthropist, and clubwoman Mary McCleod Bethune joined Hughes's and Ingram's road trip northward after they had visited Bethune-Cookman College. At every stop they made, Bethune had friends or made acquaintance with locals who gladly welcomed the trio into their homes for meals and needed rest.

This private world of support, Hughes explains, meant that they were able to avoid the awkwardness of negotiating segregated facilities close to southern highways. The exception, of course, was the inevitable need to patronize a gas station. Bethune would not cower in her request for access to use the restroom facilities. As Hughes notes, she was, in fact, critical of segregation and called it out directly in the moment, often with quite surprising responses:

> But we did have to get gas and sometimes use the gas-station rest rooms, usually one for MEN, one for LADIES—and a single one marked COLORED somewhere away out in the back for both men and women, if Negro. To the attendant at such stations, Mrs. Bethune would usually say, "Young man, do I have to avail myself of that shanty rest room away around there in the bushes?"

> If there were no whites about, the embarrassed attendant might say, "Ma'am, just use the one marked LADIES." But if the station were busy, he would indicate that the COLORED toilet was meant for her. Then Mrs. Bethune would say gently, "Aren't you ashamed, young man?"
>
> The young man would usually turn red and answer, "Yes, ma'am, I really am." (41)

After parting with Bethune, Hughes and Ingram made a stop in Columbia, South Carolina, for scheduled readings and Hughes's brief sojourn to Lower Richland to visit with Dr. Edward C. L. Adams and the interlocutors featured in Adams's collection *Congaree Sketches* as they told tall tales and folk stories and sang songs. Hughes had been told that Adams's plantation home, which had been in the family for many generations, was "run by the doctor's relatives on the colored side" (Adams 49), which heightened his confusion about the discretion taken by Adams's friend Dr. Green, a Black doctor who had transported Hughes from Columbia to the Lower Richland area.

Upon arrival, Dr. Green greeted Adams and promptly returned to his car, where he waited for Hughes. Dr. Green did not dare step foot inside Adams's home for fear of retribution from disapproving white neighbors. Fraternizing across racial lines, particularly when there existed an assumed parity in education and class status between the two southern men, risked fomenting the perception that Dr. Green had gotten out of his expected "place." On that day, to maintain peace, he elected to perform the role of chauffeur.

As they sped back to Columbia after Hughes's enjoyable visit, Dr. Green responded bluntly to Hughes's queries about the way that he had comported himself: "There are some things colored people who live here just can't do. Dr. Adams is a fine man. To him my coming in would mean nothing. But had I gone through the front door of that house as a guest and word of it got around among the white people of Columbia, it would ruin my hospital. The white drugstores might refuse to honor my prescriptions, and no more white businessmen would contribute to our building fund for the new hospital Negroes hope to erect. That is why I stayed outside, Mr. Hughes, and did not come in" (Hughes 50).

Strategically staying in one's place had its benefits, though Hughes remained troubled by the necessity of Black people making themselves smaller to survive. Hughes was certainly sympathetic to the fact that Black (auto)mobility was hazardous, having had quite a few eye-opening experiences on the road during his tour throughout the South. He had published the controversial poem "Christ in Alabama" in the December 1931 issue of *Contempo*, an unofficial student newspaper at the University of North Carolina. Hughes, as a result of the poem, was barred from housing on the campus. "Christ in Alabama" blasted the hypocritical, barbaric southern racial order, connecting the plight of African Americans with that of Jesus Christ in a fashion that was deemed sacrilegious (ironically, more so, it seems, than the lynching the poem describes). White locals were outraged; the poem's publication placed Hughes in immediate danger, and police were posted at his poetry reading, as some locals could not abide Hughes's poetic suggestion that Christ was a "bastard" or, worse in their estimation, a Black person (Hughes 46).

> Christ is a Nigger,
> Beaten and black—
> O, bare your back.
>
> Mary is His Mother
> Mammy of the South,
> Silence your Mouth.
>
> God's His Father—
> White Master above
> Grant us your love.
>
> Most holy bastard
> Of the bleeding mouth:
> Nigger Christ
> On the cross of the South.

With the Scottsboro Boys case haunting his movement across the perilous southern geography as a

Black outsider, Hughes bristled at the pettiness that undergirded segregation and the obviousness of racist white southerners' angst at somehow being overrun by Black people and culture, rightly calling this looming aspect of the region "strange, silly, [and] pathetic" (45).

* * *

Indeed, the "cross of the South" was grounded in an absurd philosophy of supremacy that had restricted the movement of Black people during slavery. In the postbellum period, methods of controlling Black people merely shifted.

And the legacy of brutality was ever present, haunting the memory of what it would mean to move forward. This is what Hughes would have known in the 1930s, the horror stories that would have accompanied him on his travels through the South.

Where, how, and when Black people could enter, move, and travel were not only constituted in segregation laws but also in everyday expectations that Black people would assume deferential postures when in the presence of white people. Throughout the South, Black people were expected to give way on sidewalks as white people approached. Local customs dictated that Black people should never look white people in the eye when speaking to them, or else they would be viewed as threatening to white authority. Even in the stillness of death, white and Black people could not share the same burial grounds.

A brief overview of South Carolina's lynching history gives a glimpse into the discomfort with which Black southerners lived and impresses on me the radicality of their decision to both stay *and* leave the South under such perilous economic and social conditions. In 1865, the Ku Klux Klan was established in Giles County, Tennessee, its charter to maintain white power at all costs.

The Klan and other domestic terrorist groups were unwilling to accept the fact of Black people moving freely about the South. Their egos bruised and threatened by what they viewed as interference from outsiders, white southerners—men and women—aimed to reinstate the antebellum-era geography of containment. They would surveil, harass, threaten, beat, and kill at their whim. With or without evidence of a crime, they would carry out vicious forms of retribution in the public square.

What terrifying times they were. Carried out by drunken misfits and the sober alike, lynchings were so mundane that vigilantes often brought their wives, children, and other family members with them to witness them enact these atrocities. Immediately held or announced in local papers, lynchings were small and large public affairs that law enforcement and the courts rarely took seriously or ventured in earnest to impede. These gruesome spectacles instilled a sense of white authority among their supporters and increasing unease among those in the Black community who were troubled by the prospect of being caught in the wrong place at the wrong time and/or being accused, "tried", and found guilty of criminal acts or social breaches that they had not committed.

Lynchings were long a regular feature of southern life but were not something that those who found them savage and distressing could ever get used to. In 1876, for instance, the paramilitary group the Red Shirts and other rifle clubs killed nearly one hundred Black people in a brutal voter-intimidation campaign of riots and murder in the mostly Black towns of Hamburg and Ellenton, South Carolina. The Red Shirts, a military faction of the Democratic Party with chapters across the South, outlined a strategy for reestablishing white power, which included the following tenets:

> We must attend every Radical meeting. Democrats must go in as large numbers as they can, and well armed, behave at first with great courtesy and as soon as their speakers begin tell them that they are liars and are only trying to mislead the ignorant Negroes. In speeches to Negroes you must remember that they can only be influenced by their fears, superstitions and cupidity. Treat them so as to show them you are the superior race and that their natural position is that of subordination to the white man. Never threaten a man individually. If he deserves to be threatened, the necessities of the times require that he

should die. A dead Radical is very harmless—a threatened Radical is often troublesome, sometimes dangerous, and always vindictive. (Facing History)

In 1889, eight Black men were arrested in connection with the murders of two white men, sparking an infamous massacre in Barnwell, South Carolina. That evening, a masked mob of vengeful killers approached the jail and tricked the jailer into opening the doors. The throng immediately rushed the door, unlocked the jail gates, and dragged the Black men and the jailer to a nearby bridge. An unwitting witness, the jailer later testified that the mob had shot the accused some 150 times over the course of five minutes.

The Black men's bodies were left on the roadside. After a postmortem check, the medical officials nonchalantly left the prone, ripped-apart bodies there for the families to claim. According to an article reprinted in newspapers nationwide, including in the *Indianapolis Journal* from December 31, 1889, "The men lay around in whatever position the surgeon had left them—on side, back or face, as the case might be. Three lay on the roadside, the others here and there among the little oaks on the side of the road, large parts of their bodies exposed and their cut and torn clothing hanging about them in a grotesque way. After the coroner's inquest, the negroes were notified that they might remove the bodies if they desired." Black leaders began imploring their community members to leave Barnwell County and other unsafe cities in South Carolina, a sentiment that would, in part, compel one of the state's first waves during the Great Migration.

Then, in 1898, the lynching of South Carolina's postmaster general outraged Americans. Appointed as the first Black postmaster in Lake City, South Carolina, Frazier B. Baker was threatened for months by local white people who did not believe that he was worthy of such a prestigious role. The disgruntled racists sent unfounded reports to the postal service, concocting complaints that purported to demonstrate Baker's inability to do his job. When their false reports did not result in the removal of Baker from his job, they set the Lake City post office building afire.

On a fateful February evening in 1898, a mob of lynchers began shooting gunfire into the makeshift post office at Baker's home. The assailants killed Baker and his two-year-old daughter, Julia, while his wife, Lavinia, two of their daughters, and their son were injured. The Bakers' other two daughters were unharmed physically. In the aftermath, the state of South Carolina refused to prosecute anyone for the murders, leaving the federal district attorney and postal inspectors to investigate and seek potential witnesses from the scared or wholly disinterested white community.

Eventually, thirteen men were arrested and charged with twenty-four counts of "conspiracy to injure and oppress Frazier B. Baker in the free exercise" of his civil rights, and the case went to trial (Smithsonian National Postal Museum). As such cases went in the South, if they ever went to trial at all, the white jury failed to convict in this instance, finding three of the men not guilty and deadlocking on the guilt or innocence of the remainder of the accused. A mistrial was declared, and the case was never revisited.

South Carolina, America, goddamn.

* * *

According to World War I military records, including draft cards and ship manifests, my great-grandfather Hampton Gilford was drafted and enlisted in June 1918. By the next month, Hampton was at Camp Jackson (now Fort Jackson) in Columbia, South Carolina, with thousands of other enlisted and drafted troops to train for combat. As part of the 92nd Division, the segregated infantry division of the United States Army, Hampton and his fellow servicemen in the 351st Regiment's field artillery formed a strategic core to provide mobile fire power during combat.

The topic of Black participation in wartime efforts has been openly controversial since before the Civil War, as the Black community debated whether enlisting in the military might demonstrate Black people's loyalty to the country and thereby convince lawmakers and elements of the hesitant white public that they were worthy of recognition as full citizens.

Returning World War I soldiers: part of Squadron A, 351st Field Artillery, returning on the transport *Louisville*. Most of these men were from Philadelphia. ("A Brief Look at African American Soldiers in the Great War," *The Unwritten Record* (blog), National Archives, February 13, 2017, local identifier 165-WW-127-2, https://unwritten-record.blogs.archives.gov/2017/02/13/a-brief-look-at-african-american-soldiers-in-the-great-war/#jp-carousel-12510)

In the April 1863 edition of *Douglass' Monthly* newspaper, the abolitionist Frederick Douglass published the essay "Why Should a Colored Man Enlist?" Douglass, who in the speech "What to the Slave Is the Fourth of July?" had famously posed and interrogated the absurdity of American independence celebrations when the institution of slavery itself was thriving, called for Black men to take a stand for their manhood and Black liberation by enlisting in the

Union army and asserting their readiness for citizenship: "You are a member of a long enslaved and despised race. Men have set down your submission to Slavery and insult, to a lack of manly courage. They point to this fact as demonstrating your fitness only to be a servile class. You should enlist and disprove the slander, and wipe out the reproach. When you shall be seen nobly defending the liberties of your own country against rebels and traitors—brass itself will blush to use such arguments imputing cowardice against you."

During World War I, the military found an unlikely recruiter in W. E. B. Du Bois, the great sociologist and cofounder of the National Association for the Advancement of Colored People (NAACP), who, too, suggested that Black men temporarily "close ranks" by putting aside their "special grievances": important and legitimate demands for equal rights to align with their countrymen and allied forces for global democracy. When the war ended in 1919 and Du Bois observed the disdainful way that far too many white people treated Black veterans, he penned the fiery essay "Returning Soldiers," which concluded with the following passionate words about the nation's failure to get beyond race and its attendant structures of oppression and violence: "We return. We return from fighting. We return fighting. Make war for democracy. We saved it in France, and by the Great Jehovah, we will save it in the United States of America, or know the reason why" (13).

At home and for US soldiers excited to read Du Bois's words abroad, that volume of the *Crisis* was held up for six days, as federal officials at the post office found it too incendiary. Just prior to the armistice, Du Bois had spent three months in 1918–19 in France in part to organize the Pan-African Congress as well as to chronicle the war by collecting stories from its African American participants. Du Bois was eager to ensure that the experiences of these men were gathered and made public, as he had been a proponent of Black American service to demonstrate their patriotism; Du Bois also was asked by men on the ground to observe their bravery and loyalty to the country, even as they suffered mistreatment by racist white military officers.

Using material that he collected firsthand, including interviews and observations, Du Bois also asked servicemen to send along their stories, diaries, photographs, and official military documentation that might be useful to the narrative that he would craft for the volume. Du Bois worked for years on *The Black Man in the World*, though it was never published in full. His accumulated archive of materials for the project, however, is quite telling.

The documents include reports that white officers downplayed displays of bravery in action, that they created stories of belligerence among Black officers and lesser-ranked soldiers, and that they attempted to convince their French counterparts that the Black officers and infantrymen were pathological and liable to rape white women if not surveilled properly. This feigned angst about supposed Black male hypersexuality and propensity for violent behavior was a repugnant carryover from slavery and insight into the levels of terror to come that would rock the nation after the war ended.

Other reports showed that while many white French citizens were initially stunned by the presence of Black people in their villages, they quickly warmed up to them and were grateful for the soldiers' presence. Some white officers and even lower-ranked soldiers, however, remained displeased by the fact that Black men could hold the same or greater rank as they. These white officers believed that the United States was a white country and that the war was the white man's war to fight and win, a white nationalist sentiment that was not new but was nonetheless enraging for Black men who were for the most part forced into the war effort, putting their already immensely precarious lives on the line. What good was it to fight for a country that barely recognized their humanity and did very little to ensure Black citizens access to life, liberty, and the pursuit of happiness?

A poem near the end of Sergeant William O. Ross and Corporal Duke L. Slaughter's *With the 351st in France (A Diary)* celebrated their victory, bravery, and honor, while acknowledging that life back at home in the United States would not be perfect. In fact, incalculable social battles were ahead:

> So here's to the Yanks of the 351st Field Artillery
> Who stood the test in No Man's Land in the fight for Democracy.
> All praise to the Allied Nations and to our own Red, White and Blue
> And now it's up to the Stars and Stripes to make it good for you.
> Your gallant deeds are writ in gold across the page of time
> And though some other mark may dim, yours may forever shine.
> Your Division is set, a dazzling star in the Nation's martial crown
> And you are the idol of the Brigade that put Bill Kaiser down. (49)

After the war ended, a new war began at home. Hundreds of reports of white boys and men harassing, beating, and lynching Black soldiers dominated the airwaves. The nationwide Red Summer of 1919 began in Charleston, South Carolina, when five white sailors retaliated against innocents after a Black man had allegedly cheated the sailors in some way. Witnessing the sailors' rampage, a Black man named Isaac Doctor began shooting at the sailors to stop their brutality. Doctor was stopped instead, killed in the streets.

When word got back to the white sailors at the Charleston Naval Yard, the narrative had become that Black people had started a riot. Some one thousand white sailors and locals descended into downtown Charleston, beating African American residents indiscriminately and destroying their homes and businesses. Six African Americans were killed, and scores of others were injured. While sixty white men were arraigned, only eight had to pay a $50 fine for carrying concealed weapons. Two others were sentenced to one year in a naval prison and were dishonorably discharged. Charleston's Black community was left to mourn and pick up the pieces in the aftermath.

In the decades that followed, there were bipolar fits and starts—moments of hope for democracy and severe despair among southern Black people as the nation fell into the financial crisis that was the Great Depression. According to the 1940 census, my great-grandfather, the World War I veteran Hampton Gilford, was out of work and his son, my grandfather Thomas, was nineteen years old, living at home with his parents and siblings and laboring at a sawmill. In 1939, Thomas was employed for twenty-four weeks and was paid a paltry $144 ($312 per year at that rate). According the US Department of Labor, the median wage or salary income in 1939 was $1,112 for white men and $460 for nonwhite men (9).

As if that were not enough economic precarity in one family, two years later, my grandfather Thomas would be off to Europe, as the country had called yet another Gilford man for duty—this time for World War II.

* * *

The markers of American mobility include the freedom of movement and the achievement of financial stability: family, education, homeownership, and increasingly in the early to mid-twentieth century, a personal automobile. For many Americans in the twentieth century, the prospect of a surer pathway to the American Dream through the perks that came along with military service by way of the Servicemen's Readjustment Act of 1944 (GI Bill) rendered enrollment in the armed forces a familial tradition. Of course, for far too many years, the respect and benefits provided to white servicemen far exceeded those that were granted to African Americans due to extreme, unchecked bias in the military. Though Black men had served in every military campaign in US history, they still were viewed as mere bodies, oftentimes planted on the front lines of war, after a short period of training, like a protective barrier to cover white soldiers, or placed in otherwise treacherous conditions.

It can be surmised, then, that the ongoing dispossession that marks so many aspects of Black life in America has not been viewed by lawmakers as any sort of emergency to address. Neither the appalling 1898 deaths of a federal postal official and his daughter nor the untold numbers of recorded and unrecorded lynchings across the nation motivated most American politicians to issue a firm and lasting legislative response to the lawlessness of white domestic terrorists in South Carolina or elsewhere. In light of this negligence at the federal and state levels, the journalist and activist Ida B. Wells and later the NAACP initiated a full-scale antilynching campaign in the early twentieth century that involved letters, newspaper articles, pamphlets, and legal cases in the courts to rally for official legislation against the barbarous acts executed by white Americans.

In 1918, the Republican US Representative Leonidas C. Dyer of Missouri moved to address the issue. He proposed a federal antilynching bill that would make lynching a federal felony, with explicit sentences for those who were found guilty as well as for law enforcement officers who aided and abetted these crimes. The proposed bill held southern states accountable, as they rarely investigated or prosecuted lynching cases because their agencies were often infested with local officials who sympathized with the offenders, if they were not eager participants themselves.

One hundred years later, Congress has still not passed antilynching legislation to make lynching a federal hate crime, though hundreds of iterations of such a bill have come up, including a promising consideration in 1922 that was ultimately tamped down by Democratic southern senators via filibuster. The

Senate unanimously passed the Justice for Victims of Lynching Act in 2018, but it died because it was not passed by the House of Representatives. As of 2020, a revised version of the 2018 bill, the Emmett Till Antilynching Act, awaits congressional approval.

What is the value of Black life in America?

* * *

Discussions of American slavery and resistance, Black migration, and mobility became a brief, though significant, part of the congressional record in May 1968 via the inclusion of the following statement by the businessman Frank Threatt, owner of the Congaree Iron and Steel Company (CISCO) in Lower Richland: "I want to point out that we are now operating an underground railroad from the North to the South. We are slipping colored people back to us. I have a list of names here that we have slipped out of big cities and we have got them back home. We understand their talk. We understand their needs, and we are going to try our best as a small business in the South to take some of the pressure off the northern cities by the operation of this underground railroad" (US Congress 13). Threatt had traveled to Washington, DC, to give a statement before the Subcommittee on Financing and Investment of the Select Committee on Small Business. He thanked the Small Business Administration and the Rural Electrification Administration for their approval of his loans and their mentorship along the way. Most heartening was his enthusiastic championing of the goodness, intellect, and hard-working nature of the Black people of the Lower Richland/Congaree area.

Threatt matters to my story because the company he founded—the ability for wealth and stability that it offered—played such a major part in what upward mobility would mean to the Black Americans where I am from (you will find his name in chapter 4 as well). It is fitting, perhaps, that not only did the jobs he created matter, but the nature of those jobs—working with steel—enabled his employees to actually craft the material of American mobility and uplift. My grandfather, the railroad worker "Railroad Man"/"Steel Man" and World War II veteran worked for CISCO for some time. When I think more broadly about the hope offered by the company, I see the return, and the rewriting, of the nineteenth-century history of Black laborers building the infrastructure of America.

Threatt opened CISCO in 1957 and employed some 425 people within a decade; 90 percent of his workers, including several supervisors, were African American, many of whom had previously worked underpaid jobs on the railroad and as farmers. Along with his overdone "underground railroad to economic freedom in the South" rhetoric, Threatt's articulated mission was steeped in business-speak, but the main thrust is that he wanted to work with other businesspeople, lawmakers, and community leaders to change negative perceptions of the area.

The transcript and some of the responses from the members of Congress suggest that Threatt perhaps was a bit too chatty and effusive in his praise of Black southerners for the lawmakers' liking, but I remain struck by his recognition of and insistence on Black humanity on the official congressional record. Threatt had been invited to testify before Congress because of an article published six months prior in the December 15, 1967, issue of *Life* magazine. The issue features a story pegged as one of redemption and rural renewal entitled "Frank Threatt's Quiet Drive on Prejudice." It highlights CISCO's policy to recruit Black convicts from chain gangs and the company's refusal to further punish those with criminal pasts so long as they were willing to come to work on time and work hard.

Threatt employed others without criminal records, of course, but his success with rehabilitating those often relegated to the severe margins of society after they were released from prison was viewed as unique and instructive for other businesses across the United States. Threatt had established his company in 1957 with three Black workers and later with the labor of fifty men with whom he dug ditches and built the plant. After a visit and tour of Lower Richland with Threatt, US Agriculture Secretary Orville Freeman asserted that CISCO was a "picture-book example of what needs to be done across the nation" and lauded Threatt for his efforts ("Frank Threatt's" 39). Threatt explained about the people who worked for him, "Most of them are basically good people," and he observed that the white people in the Congaree area were "beginning to understand that Negroes learn as quickly and are just as dependable and that all they need is some help, some direction—and the best way to do that is to make sure that they can become constructively employed" (39).

Life featured three African American men who were becoming more upwardly mobile because of their work at CISCO: Willie Garrick's new life was shown opposite the clapboard home in which he was raised. The dilapidated wood structure paled in comparison to his new home and automobile under the carport. As a superintendent of production, Garrick earned close to $10,000 a year, purchased stock in the company often, and saved for his children's education. Lewis Robertson, an assembly line foreman, bought a home and was saving to build an even nicer one on the forty acres that he had purchased in the area. He had sent his wife to nursing school and was saving money for his son's education. Sam McKnight was pictured in his home, where he showed off the new wall-to-wall carpeting that he purchased for his wife for their anniversary. McKnight was presently saving to purchase a car and declared that he wanted all of his children to attend college: "I don't want them to come up the way I came up—my hope is to make it easier for them" (42).

Threatt's fairly progressive vision about race and work was an anomaly in the era, and he admitted that it had taken him some time to evolve personally. Eager to participate in combat during World War II, Threatt took on the challenge of leading what he referred to as an "eight-ball" unit, an all-Black company of men with persistent disciplinary issues. Theretofore, Threatt was admittedly racist and thought of African Americans as inferior beings. Though he struggled to assert himself with the men, he went on to earn their respect, and they all exited the war highly decorated for their valor. Threatt remarked about his own redemption, "The war taught me that Negroes were people like anybody else and not a race" (48). When Threatt was again called to serve—this time in the Korean War—his neighbor Willie Wilson, who had been born in a slave cabin behind Threatt's home at the time, protected and cared for Threatt's farm for free while he was away, leading to a years-long work and friendly relationship between the two men.

As Threatt established CISCO in Lower Richland, he received an unwanted visit from the supremacist White Citizens' Council, whose purpose was to actively reject all efforts to desegregate the South, via violence, menace, economic boycotts, and the firing of Black people and their allies from their jobs. Threatt was referred to as a "nigger lover" after his refusal to join the Lower Richland chapter, and he experienced three instances of intimidation by night riders who shot into his home to announce their presence. He convincingly returned fire in the third instance and remained steadfast in his articulated purpose to ensure that he and other proponents of Lower Richland could lure Black southerners back home. Threatt understood that Black southerners' northward migrations had not always been financially beneficial or socially accepted and that Lower Richland needed to build more infrastructure, homes, and educational and professional opportunities to make it an appealing option. This was the only way to show and prove that a robust future was to be had there for subsequent generations.

***

Everybody in the country knew Grandma Isabell's gold-colored, cabbed GMC pickup truck. It was an odd vehicle choice for a woman, some thought, but that massive gas-guzzler, which belonged to her late husband, gave her the ability to haul her goods and her six grandchildren when needed. I spent untold hours traveling the thirty or so minutes to run errands in Columbia or to accompany Grandma as she cleaned the homes of some of East Columbia's white professional class. As we sprinted up and down narrow and dusty dirt roads to deliver her Blair and Watkins catalog products to faithful customers, I would halfway listen to whatever was playing on the AM dial or simply the static, because Grandma did not abide secular music.

Grandma was often in the kind of deep thought that comes along with traveling familiar roads, and I, just a little girl, was probably thinking about toys or sweets or missing my mama. I remember the stickiness of summer leather seats and the fear of returning to the sunbaked and thoroughly heated-through truck after one of Grandma's jobs. The coolness remained in the blue Coleman cooler, which held our lunch for the day: legitimately yummy leftovers of comfort food, sandwiches, or, during leaner weeks, the dreaded meal of cold Vienna sausages and saltine crackers. I usually only perked up when we neared a large farm with neatly planted crops. I found inexplicable joy in turning my head slightly to the right and holding my eyes open for as long as possible. What a joy to witness the optical illusion created as we sped past rows of corn and other crops.

I drive through Lower Richland in my early-40s with a different set of hopes and expectations. On travels home these days, it is as if I am a teenager again, asking permission to take my mother's car somewhere. My requests are for the go-ahead to wander alone . . . to be free to imagine the world of my recent and distant ancestors on hallowed ground. Mama always says yes now, calmed, in part, by my maturity and also by the chance to watch her grandson without me hovering or distracting him from her.

In these travels through Lower Richland, I have driven past the point of comfort down familiar and unfamiliar pathways. On quiet roads, being in the only car for miles raises my anxiety regarding the possibility of not knowing what to do if I lose control or if the car somehow stalls, stranding me between two sides of a swampy forest. Fear has gotten the best of me, too, as I point the car straight and in full control yet into the unknown because I'd never been on a particular side road, dirt road, or secondary highway. Drivers who are used to a road's particularities—its narrowing, the ways that curves tighten and become completely blind to those who pass infrequently—know how to compensate. But when the FM radio statics out, one's cell phone loses signal, and tree canopies darken the road (even on the sunniest days), the feeling is quite haunting.

My aforementioned unannounced trip to Wavering Place Plantation was a bust. As I approached the driveway onto the property, I slowed the car significantly to ensure that I was turning into the correct entrance. I had hoped for a tour or perhaps permission to walk the grounds informally. A growling, souped-up black Ford F-250 pickup truck came thundering up behind me in a severe tailgate, so I pulled into the plantation's small driveway, where I immediately noticed the locked gate.

I used my cell phone to visit the plantation's website and noticed the owners' promise that the plantation was "more than a venue, but an experience." A history of the family is included as well, which celebrates much of the family's history of plantation ownership, especially that of the Adams family patriarch Joel Adams, who was an officer during the American Revolution and was fondly known as "Joel of All" because of his twenty-five thousand acres of plantation land in the Lower Richland area. Wavering Place was bought most recently by Weston Adams III and Robert Adams VI, ensuring that the property has remained in the Adams family since 1768. Among the antebellum edifices that survive at Wavering Place are outbuildings from the early 1800s, including the kitchen house and double slave dwelling, a smokehouse, plantation office, and a barn. To meet demands and subdue the critiques that abound about businesses like theirs, the current owners state that they are working on a database that captures the traces of the enslaved "artisans, craftsmen, and workers who built and tended" and that they are willing to provide available records to African Americans conducting genealogical research about their enslaved ancestors.

Located in Eastover, Wavering Place is a national historical landmark and received an easement from the Congaree Land Trust for preservation and conservation. Yet, no matter how gussied up this nineteenth-century Greek Revival home has become during its two centuries of existence, the plantation cannot shake its history as a site of slavery. Its current use, ever popular in the region to satiate the desires of tourists who are eager to experience the affluence of the Old South, gives me pause.

Today, Wavering Place has fashioned itself as a special site for solitude or events, one at which a writer could, for several hundred dollars a night, reserve a room to rest and partake of a continental breakfast while preparing a manuscript. It is a popular wedding venue that puts one in the mind of other iterations in Charleston, Savannah, and New Orleans. What is it about this particular aspect of the past that is most attractive as a backdrop for those consumed by the idea of the antebellum southern romance? Brides and grooms can become principal actors in the photographed plantation fantasy, exiting their ceremony with the stately plantation home, exquisitely kept grounds, weeping willows, and magnolia trees in place behind them.

And perhaps they come for the possibility of time travel. For tens of thousands of dollars, one can purchase a half day of pretense: a closeness to the land and the attendant historical wealth that they may or may not have been born into, as well as the closeness to nature in the outer reaches of town. But never the atrocity. What does it mean for the Adams family to continue to prosper from this gruesome history? How dare anyone recite a history of a complicated place like Lower Richland absent the horror?

***

I grew up singing contemporary choir songs alongside Negro spirituals and old hymns in church. Songs such as "Ezekiel Saw the Wheel" and "We Are Climbing Jacob's Ladder" contained messages about ascension and had nurtured previous generations spiritually. But our ancestors and elders also recognized the necessity of an on-the-ground philosophy for negotiating the world. My grandfather Thomas Butler, Grandma Isabell's second husband, was a deacon in a lively Pentecostal church, where it was normal for church members to unabashedly and spontaneously assert their praises to the Lord, move about in a trance-like state called shouting, and speak in tongues. On a fateful day in November 1995, my grandfather rose from his pew to sing the lead vocals of a song entitled "Running for My Life."

The song, like other spirituals, contains interrelated meanings regarding hope, grace, and the opportunity to truly live after physical death. I imagine that for my grandfather, it also spoke directly to his unwavering Christian faith as well as to the idea of escaping to an elsewhere that was better than life here on earth—an otherwise existence. They sang,

> I'm running for my life, I'm running for my life.
> I'm running for my life, I'm running for my life.
> If anybody asks you, what's the matter with me,
> Tell them that I'm saved and sanctified,
> Holy Ghost filled and I've been baptized.
> I've got Jesus on the inside and I'm running for
>   my life.

At the close of the song, my grandfather suddenly collapsed and then transitioned hours later. Born in 1917, he had seen American oppression and terror in ways that haunt and reverberate in our moment; he had prayed with fervor for basic civil rights for which we, perhaps, will never have to pray; he had fled to New York City and then back to South Carolina for a better chance at life. The thought that he has journeyed to the home of his imagination sustains me, even as I lament that Black movements in life are perpetually restricted.

4

BUS

It's not the bus, it's us.
—Julian Bond

The civil-rights-related bus agitation you might think of took place on a Cleveland Avenue bus in Montgomery, Alabama, in December 1955—Rosa Parks's staunch refusal to give up her seat to a white patron. Buses were the site of a great deal of civil disobedience in the 1950s and 1960s. But prior to Jo Ann Robinson's organization of the Montgomery Bus Boycott and Rosa Parks's and Claudette Colvin's well-known defiance of southern segregationist bus laws, South Carolina was the site of a similar protest.

On June 22, 1954, twenty-one-year-old Sarah Mae Flemming, a domestic worker from Eastover, South Carolina, boarded a bus in nearby Columbia, unaware that the seat she had taken was not in the colored section. The driver immediately berated Flemming; embarrassed, she tried to make a quick exit through the bus's front door. But according to the city's segregationist policies, Flemming, unlike the white patrons she was following, was not allowed to exit that way. The driver punched Flemming for what he viewed as her refusal to follow the racialized aspects of the transportation ordinance.

Rosa Parks's protest led to a monumentally successful boycott and lawsuit. Sarah Mae Flemming was not as fortunate. In the case *Flemming v. South Carolina Electric and Gas*, she and her attorneys argued that South Carolina Electric and Gas, which operated the city's buses, had violated Flemming's Fourteenth Amendment right to equal protection under the law. The case was dismissed by a federal district judge, while the Fourth Circuit Court of Appeals reversed the federal decision and remanded the case for further proceedings. In its next phase, the case went back before the initial judge and was summarily dismissed. The South Carolina Supreme Court refused to hear the case.

Flemming's relatively unknown yet brave attempt to breach bus protocols was a preview of the coming explosion of civil rights battles across the South, including bus boycotts and Freedom Rides, that challenged segregationist policies on public transportation. It most especially highlighted the ways that civil disobedience could be used by anyone willing to challenge the order of the day.

Over the first half of the twentieth century, American cities began to develop modern public bus systems, often giving up on street cars or subway systems to do so. The year 1940 was the first when national bus ridership exceeded street railway ridership. The addition of public buses offered everyday citizens mobility and convenience—particularly for working-class workers who could not afford automobiles. Public buses meant a public with more control over where to work and where to live—a public that could move between work and home securely and on time. These were needs that African Americans had struggled for many years to meet. But for Black riders, the promise of affordability, access, and safety was unevenly delivered. What might it cost to travel by bus?

For Black public bus riders, untold dangers and worry took their toll: the intimacy of traveling at the hands of a white stranger who may have held resentments; the intimacy of sitting so closely to other passengers who may or may not have had good intentions; or the off chance that one's accidental glance, touch, or mere presence might have set off some sort of trouble.

The stakes were just as high or higher for Black schoolchildren. School busing was intended to usher them into a more egalitarian society. Proponents of busing believed that Black children's access to schools with better resources would give them and successive generations more of a chance at realizing prosperous futures.

But as activists found out firsthand, segregationists, from lawmakers to laypeople, were determined to counter all progressive-minded forms of protest and ensuing legislation, and this reactionary spirit would inflect the school busing debates that came later. In 1957, the infamous Dixiecrat and segregationist Senator Strom Thurmond of South Carolina filibustered the passage of a civil rights package, speaking for twenty-four hours and eighteen minutes and demonstrating his commitment to the 1956 Southern Manifesto, which outlined southern lawmakers' resistance to integration. On the US Senate floor three years later, Thurmond defiantly dared northern lawmakers to pass civil rights legislation that intruded on the South's racist ways, unmoved by the prospect that there could be profound improvements in Americans' collective educational and financial mobility:

> And these gentlemen who would remake the South might as well accept the fact, at long last, that—despite all the superficial changes, the new industry, the factories, the superhighways, the glass-fronted suburban shopping centers—the South is going to continue to be, in its essentials, very different from the North. The South, in short, is here to stay. . . . We, the white people of the South serve warning now upon you of the North, that what you are about to try to do to the Southern Negro, in this new and futile attempt to reshape the South in the Northern image, will be sternly and steadfastly resisted by us. (22–25)

A heinous feature of this moment was the fact that so many Americans were willing to share their racist bile and acts of violent retribution without shame or fear of consequence. In 1961, for instance, Black college students from Allen University and Benedict College protested, sat in, and were arrested at the Greyhound bus terminal in Columbia after peacefully contesting the company's failure to offer equal service to its customers. On February 9, 1968, students from Orangeburg's South Carolina State University and Claflin University united to protest the recently built, segregated All-Star Bowling Lanes. Bolstered by members of the National Guard, who were on edge because of the perceived "threat" posed by black militants, and empowered by the governor, South Carolina highway patrolmen opened fire on two hundred Black student protestors, killing three young people and wounding twenty-eight others. While nine of the seventy highway patrolmen at the scene were tried in federal court for imposing summary punishment without due process of the law, the officers claimed that they feared for *their* own lives, as the refrain intones today during instances of alleged police brutality. The twenty-three-member grand jury refused to indict the officers. Cleveland Sellers, a Howard University graduate and native of Denmark, South Carolina, was the only student protester arrested, as he was viewed by the governor and law enforcement as a militant Black Power nationalist who had riled up the other students with extremist beliefs. Convicted of rioting at the bowling alley, Sellers was sentenced to one year of hard labor.

These acts of violence against students took place only six months before my mother entered South Carolina State University as a freshman. The 1970 Lamar Riot over school busing was the next in a series of significant instances of transportation- and desegregation-related unrest in South Carolina. The state's educational system would be impacted forever.

* * *

I have not always expressed my love and longing for home outwardly, in the way that young people sometimes feign indifference to their roots in the service of asserting their belief that they are somehow *grown* and ready to be on their own as soon as they turn eighteen years old. Throughout my childhood, my teenage years especially, Lower Richland High School was on the news for some negative reason or another—underperformance on standardized tests, fights between students, always something (real or otherwise)—which certainly cast a shadow over people's perceptions of us. During my senior year, I won a school-wide prize for a short essay in which I railed against the media for its damaging coverage and lack of direct contact with our students, teachers, and administration. I knew that sincere engagements with us would have offered the media and its viewers a fuller story—that narratives mattered—even when I could not recite the long history of racialized precarity in the region or the societal structures that made it so.

No matter what was said about us, I was never ever ashamed of being *country* or from the country. And I certainly was never ashamed of being Black. I realized that there were issues that the media did not dare broach, including the differences in the ways that students traversed Lower Richland and how the historical circumstances that were largely created by adults affected the ways that students related to one another across race and class.

Growing up, I mostly attended schools in the Lower Richland area. A small group of my Black friends and I were bused to majority-white, middle-class elementary schools with gifted and talented programs and generally better resources. By middle school, I enrolled in the majority–African American Hopkins Middle School, which had a gifted and talented program and from which I received a pretty good education. But this school was also where the violent legacies of slavery and Jim Crow haunted us students in a curious, unexpected way. Indeed, there often was a palpable thickness to the air we breathed—a wretched moodiness to it.

As an adult, I've often pondered on the history of race riots in the public schools in Richland County during its belated period of school desegregation, including the actions of Lower Richland High School's renowned football coach Mooney Player, who allegedly abused Black students and created the "Deadline '72" campaign to halt school desegregation in the region in the early 1970s. As students in Lower

Our Young People Are Coming Home....

What happens to a small rural town when the local rural electric system helps start an enlightened and progressive industry?

In Congaree, South Carolina, what happened has been described as "an economic and sociological miracle."

Ten years ago Congaree was going nowhere, but its young people were—to New York, Detroit, Philadelphia, Cincinnati, Los Angeles, Chicago and Washington. Many of them were untrained for productive jobs and most of them added to the burdens of the cities.

Then a new local industry, the Congaree Iron & Steel Company, began operations with the help of the Tri-County Electric Cooperative and a Small Business Administration loan.

Now the company employs more than 400 people, most of whom once fit precisely the definitions of "unemployables" or "hard-core unemployed."

"We have reversed the trend," says President Frank Threatt, "and our young people are coming home. . . ."

The town of Congaree and its surrounding area reflect the progress of the people. Two new schools and 27 classroom additions have been built, 75 new homes, three filling stations, a bakery, a small shopping center, a new post office, a machine shop, two new laundries, two new churches, a restaurant, several country stores. Property values have tripled, the tax base has increased five times over, and the company feeds two million dollars a year in payroll and local purchases into the economy.

All over the country the rural electric systems are making the development of the areas they serve a number one priority. The job they're doing has beneficial results far beyond their own borders.

For it is inescapably true that the crisis in the cities and the economic decline of rural areas have the common denominator of poverty and lack of opportunity.

Congaree is just one example of what the rural electrics are doing about it. We like to have our young people come back home.

<u>Everybody</u> benefits **AMERICA'S *Consumer-Owned* RURAL ELECTRIC SYSTEMS**

Congaree Iron and Steel advertisement: "Our Young People Are Coming Home." (*Harper's Magazine*, May 1, 1968, 24, ProQuest)

Richland, we—the Black students who desegregated the school in the 1970s as well as my cohort that came along twenty years later—existed in the shadows of former plantations, where many of our family members had been enslaved and, after slavery, where many of them toiled in a kind of neoslavery under the sharecropping system. I was born in 1978, a member of my maternal family's first generation of children born after the legislative end of the twentieth century's civil rights movement.

A pair of violent refrains marked my three years at Hopkins Middle. Students would occasionally arrive at school and feel something in the air. We would whisper to one another, "I can feel a fight" or "There's going to be a riot," meaning a fight between boys, white and black. These proclamations were probably complex holdovers from the volatile moment when Lower Richland area schools finally desegregated in the 1970s and were the unfortunate site of violent episodes instigated by those who were resistant to change. By my middle school years of 1989–92, neither the literature nor the social studies curricula included memorable, in-depth units about slavery or the civil rights movement. I still do not know exactly how we students were armed with the language of "riots" and "race" and why our boys were prompted to act out in the ways that they did. But I do know that much of the administration and faculty members were complicit: their willful and perhaps unintentional glossing over of our shared histories, their refusal to address the historical truths and their ensuing silence, helped create and maintain a precarious terrain that we students were too young and too naive to negotiate alone.

* * *

While parental debates over busing were exploding across the South in the late 1960s, the economic situation in Lower Richland among Black and white residents was on the upswing due, in part, to CISCO's rapid growth and influence in the community. Frank Threatt's popularity as a small-business wonder, however, peaked in 1969. Magazine and newspaper profiles and national television programs celebrated Threatt, describing him as a moderate racist turned compassionate "pied piper" who lured busloads of Black people back home to the South. For many observers, Threatt's business model and personal reflections about race were shifting the narrative about the South's backwardness, and the media seemed to clamor for evidence that a future indeed was to be had in the region. According to a speech given by J. A. Baker, the assistant secretary of the US Department of Agriculture, the December 4, 1967, issue of the *National Observer* declared, "A dying region has been revived. Negro tenant farmers, who constitute 85 percent of the population in the area, have stopped their steady migration to urban slums. Now they find training and work at home. Some who did move away have returned to work at

CISCO. Welfare payments in the region have been reduced" (14).

The previously mentioned *Life* magazine article included a picture of Threatt standing "on the filigreed porch of his 200-year-old plantation house," an agreed-on pose that the photographer staged to highlight Threatt's economic success as well as the social progress in the region (44). Threatt's proud face is lit by the sun, and the low-angle perspective figures him as a powerful hero to whom the reader should look up. The staging of the image also unwittingly brings into view the ways that American capitalism relies on the exploitation of Black laborers, even as certain members of Lower Richland and surrounding counties experienced improvements to their livelihoods. The truth is that one booming business alone could not save a region, even though, as Senator John Speakman of Alabama highlighted in the "rural renewal" hearings, a Chamber of Commerce algorithm for understanding the impact of business on American communities showed that Lower Richland was exceeding expectations fourfold. He praised Threatt for his accomplishments thusly:

> This [algorithm] relates to 100 new workers, and yours would be 425. It says 100 new workers coming into a community means 359 more people in that community, 91 more school children, that is the average, I guess, down in your area it is more than that, $710,000 more personal income, 100

more households, a $229,000 increase in bank deposits, three more retail establishments, 97 more passenger cars registered, 65 more employed in nonmanufacturing; that is, your service stations and your laundries, and service organizations, $331,000 more retail sales per year. Now, you multiply all of those figures by four and a quarter, and it draws quite a picture as to what the growth of your business has meant there in Congaree. (US Congress 19)

Similarly impressed with Threatt's business accomplishments, the Ford Foundation had awarded CISCO a high-risk, low-yield $1 million grant in 1968 that underwrote a profit-sharing plan for hundreds of workers in Lower Richland ("Ford"). Unfortunately, these financial investments were not sustainable. By 1972, CISCO was in the process of reorganization under the direction of a court-appointed trustee (*Aiken Standard*, December 14, 1971, 2). It is unclear what occurred in the years after CISCO's most profitable era. Perhaps the mild recession of 1969–70, caused in part by the market's reaction to the Vietnam War and the draft carrying off workers to combat, together with the Small Business Administration's many scandals and upheavals, national and international competition, and an overall untenable business model, led to CISCO's bankruptcy. The effects in Lower Richland were probably swift, with a demoralized public worried about its well-being and forced busing legislation threatening to upend the racialized traditions in the secluded community.

In hindsight, Threatt's business, which was bolstered by local and federal loans, had risen mightily in the middle of the United States' civil rights fight, in which protests across the nation had led to some promising outcomes as it related to the slow defeat of Jim Crow. As CISCO failed, Lower Richland families, too, faced new obstacles. My grandfather Thomas Gilford had worked as a welder at CISCO, and Grandma Isabell labored as a laundress at Fort Jackson, an army installation in Columbia. This period of financial uncertainty must have been disheartening and frightening for the entire community, as the very company that had attracted new investments in the area had folded. New anxieties, too, spread across Lower Richland: violent skirmishes over busing and integration compounded an already uncertain economic situation for many families. Now, their children's educational futures were at risk.

***

On March 9, 1970, some two hundred white men and women in Lamar, South Carolina, overturned two buses in which Black children sat. Angered by the federal mandate for Darlington County to desegregate its schools immediately, the Citizens for Freedom of Choice protested the presence of Black students at the local schools and rioted, without much interference from the law enforcement officers on the scene.

Armed with ax handles, chains, bricks, rocks, and sticks, the mobs busted out the buses' windows, dismantled their engines, and fought with the police when they finally attempted to stop the miscreants. While there were no arrests on the day of the riot, seven men were taken into custody the next day. Harry Dent, a political strategist and one of the cocreators of President Richard Nixon's infamous Southern Strategy, spoke in the aftermath of the Lamar Riot to laud Nixon's hands-off approach to desegregation. He argued that leaving the response to southern law enforcement and elected officials would avoid the creation of "another Little Rock" (Dent)—the famous collision between state and nation in which the Arkansas National Guard was used to block Black students from walking into Little Rock High School and President Dwight D. Eisenhower intervened by sending in federal troops to escort the nine students into the school safely.

Arthur Stanley of the local NAACP chapter spoke of a plan to demand that the federal government investigate the riots, as the failure of the small-town officials to charge more members of the mob was a "conspiracy in Darlington County to deny Black and white people of their rights" (Best and Stanley; Bryant). In addition to the failure to charge those who were involved, most media narratives about the riot erroneously reported that while the mob indeed overturned buses, no children were on board at the time they were tipped over. Upon the sentencing of some of the men, Judge Wade Weatherford commented to them, in part, "You are not criminals, but you have violated the law and therefore must be punished. As long as we're human, we're going to be imperfect" ("Lamar"). Judge Weatherford went on to chastise the men for their acts, which had damaged the state's reputation on a national scale. He seems unwilling to identify them as criminals, even though they meet the definition by having broken the law, because he believes their feelings about the immediacy of the changes instituted via busing were legitimate. But it is hard to give credit to the idea that desegregation was really so sudden. It was sixteen years after *Brown v. Board of Education*.

William F. McIllwain of *Esquire* magazine traveled to Lamar and surrounding towns to retrace the morning of the riot as well as to take the pulse of the region. He immediately noted that Black and white parents were hesitant to bus their children, particularly in the middle of the school year. Most white parent members of the Citizens for Freedom of Choice organization stated that they were not against integration, but McIllwain's interviews with white locals outside of that group, which had leveled unfounded complaints that Black teachers were ill prepared to teach white children, offered even less-sanitized responses to inquiries about their stance on busing.

As was the case across the South and in other parts of the country where white flight had seen white families fleeing to the suburbs and placing their children into private schools to avoid integration, the violent pushback from students who were upset about busing led to the implementation of severe changes to school schedules: shorter school days, the elimination of recess, and abbreviated lunch periods. Yet, according to McIllwain's teenage informants, the fears of widespread rioting or harassment did not appear to match most of the students' intentions. The angst had been stoked by their intolerant parents. McIllwain astutely demonstrates this in his extended juxtaposition of a range of openly racist (or dog-whistling) Lamar residents with that of more open-minded Black and white teenagers:

> Henry Alford, the black student who was driving one of the school buses that was attacked, saw white friends in the mob, boys he had played basketball with. "But I don't blame it so much on them," Henry says. "Their parents were pushing them. The parents were the ones who were stirring up hard feelings."
>
> Mike Windam, seventeen, is a sandy-haired football player who stayed in Lamar High. He wanted to, and his parents wanted him to. He plans to go to the University of South Carolina and study pharmacy. "About half of our senior class didn't come back," Mike says. "Lots of parents around here wanted to keep their children

out, but the children wanted to come back. That's why some of them were out so long. They finally talked their parents into letting them come back."

Gordon Cole, Lamar High principal, agrees that this parent-student struggle went on. He thinks many parents brought great pressure on their children at the time to drop out of the public schools and go to private schools.

"If it was left up to the students," he says, "I could take my buses in there and clear out those private schools. I've talked to the students and I know how they feel."

At the time Cole is speaking, attendance figures at Lamar Elementary and Lamar High show precisely what happened to those two schools. There are sixty whites and a hundred seventy-five blacks at Lamar Elementary, missing three hundred whites who are supposed to be there. There are a hundred fifteen whites and a hundred fifty-five blacks at Lamar High, missing a hundred seventy-five whites who are supposed to be there. (At Spaulding Elementary and Spaulding High, there are no white children. Under the new integration plan, a hundred twenty were to have transferred to Spaulding; not one did.) In all of Darlington County, approximately fifteen hundred white students dropped out of the public schools. An estimated [one] thousand of them went to private schools or to schools in nearby counties. Five hundred apparently went to no school at all. That is a hard indictment of Darlington County parents. But perhaps parents will change. (162–63)

* * *

The *Swann v. Charlotte-Mecklenburg Board of Education* (1971) case led to the implementation of federal policies to use busing to eliminate the de facto school segregation that existed for nearly two decades after the passage of *Brown v. Board of Education* (1954). Busing, the mandated transportation of schoolchildren to schools within or outside their districts to promote racial balance, was a largely unpopular practice nationwide. It posed inconveniences to many families whose children were required to leave community schools and travel, usually by foot or by bus, many miles to newly assigned schools. And some white parents worried about the prospect of their children being *forced* to learn alongside Black students at schools outside their home communities. Parents of all races resisted busing for various uncertainties, with a large percentage of white parents across the South electing to place their children in segregated private and parochial schools instead.

The struggles that Black parents faced when attempting to secure a decent education for their children are staggering. In South Carolina, battles over educating Black children and school inequality had been ongoing since Reconstruction, with major cases tried in state and federal courts for much of the twentieth century. Levi and Viola Pearson, for instance, filed a lawsuit against the Clarendon County Board of Education in 1947, alleging that the board did not provide adequate transportation for Black children to safely travel to local schools. The Pearsons' three children had been forced to walk nine miles to school, leading the Pearsons to work with other parents and concerned members of their community to raise funds to purchase a used school bus for $900. Because the bus broke down often and thus needed repairs, the strapped community appealed to the Board of Education for assistance. The county, which had provided thirty school buses for white children and none for Black children, refused their demands. Unsurprisingly, the *Pearson v. Clarendon County Board of Education* case was dismissed but for a trumped-up reason: the Pearsons were not deemed taxpayers in the school district in Summerton due to a newly created property law.

In cases throughout the South, conservative, segregationist judges continued to throw out lawsuits after cursory reviews. Local Black activists including professionals, everyday people, and attorneys continued to agitate in the courts, despite the known uphill battles that they were facing, eventually gaining the attention of national civil rights organizations including the NAACP.

According to the South Carolina Education Survey Committee's report *Public Schools of South Carolina*, the state of South Carolina spent $368.94 per white student and $66.77 per Black student toward school facilities in 1946–47, which, along with underpaid, overworked Black teachers, resulted in a degree of hopelessness, a stark lack of educational resources, and dilapidated school buildings in the Black community (86).

The fight for equal schools in Clarendon County went on for several years, with the most successful attempt made by a group of twenty parents in the *Briggs v. Elliott* case, which went after the president of the Clarendon County school board for his implementation of segregationist policies. Thurgood Marshall served as the lead counsel for the NAACP Legal Defense Fund alongside the South Carolina–based attorney Harold Boulware. While the US district court's three-justice panel did not find that schools should be desegregated, they were convinced by testimony about the psychological impact that segregation had on Black students' mental health and self-actualization and ordered the commencement of sincere attempts at school equalization.

Briggs v. Elliott eventually became one of several cases that were combined to compose *Brown v. Board of Education*, which Thurgood Marshall went on to argue successfully in 1954, convincing the Supreme Court justices of the unconstitutionality of segregated schools. South Carolina schools, like those throughout the South, though, did not desegregate right away—their defiance made possible via several legal loopholes and the reluctance or sheer unwillingness of the federal government to place too much pressure on state governments. Many white parents assumed that the curricula at their children's schools would become less rigorous to accommodate Black students' supposed ignorance, while Black parents were apprehensive about the treatment, care, and education that their children would receive from white teachers.

The ways that those who were opposed to integration reacted as busing policies were slowly enforced is a shameful indictment of closed-minded South Carolinians and assists me in better understanding my own education in the state's public schools beginning in 1983. Early on, I began to understand the ways that race and class inflected relations inside the classroom. I took my place in gifted and talented and college-prep classrooms that were taught almost exclusively by white teachers and occupied by a disproportionate number of white students. My educational experiences in 1980s–1990s Lower Richland were palimpsests, engagements that were indelibly marked by the recent and distant histories that had anticipated our arrival.

* * *

Buses were used by children, by protesters, and also by counterprotesters. In August 1971, Black students from the Lower Richland area traveled to the administrative offices of Richland County School District

Students protest the closing of Hopkins High School, August 10, 1971. (Whitney Black, The State Media Company [Columbia, SC], Richland County Public Library, Box 48, Hopkins High students picketing, 4E-0461, https://cdm16817.contentdm.oclc.org/digital/collection/p16817coll21/id/6174/rec/44)

One to protest the closing of their all-Black Hopkins High School and the forced integration with Lower Richland High School. The next month, a group of adult neo-Nazis arrived by bus to the South Carolina State House with the intention of creating a spectacle and meeting with Governor John C. West about their segregationist beliefs and the law.

Emblazoned with the phrases "White Power," "Gas Race Mixers," and "Boycott Busing" as well as several swastikas and Confederate flags, the neo-Nazi bus was photographed by local newspapers, which indirectly helped the white supremacists advertise their message and potentially recruit new

Neo-Nazi bus at the State House, September 9, 1971. (Larry Cagle, The State Media Company [Columbia, SC], Richland County Public Library, Box 48, Nazi party members at Gov. office, 4E-0623, https://cdm16817.contentdm.oclc.org/digital/collection/p16817coll21/id/6148/rec/6)

members. The men deboarded their bus outfitted in button-down uniform shirts with swastikas on their sleeves and marched toward the state capitol. Although Governor West declined to meet with them, their desire to shock, intimidate, and recruit via the media attention was met and probably exceeded, as white parents across South Carolina were enraged by the further intrusion of what they deemed to be northern ways on their customs and as Black parents feared the violent unknown, haunted by the atrocities of the not-too-distant past.

There is a social media site for Lower Richland High School alumni that I visit from time to time. The members include those who graduated from the 1960s to the present, and it brings me immense joy to see just how beloved the school is. Lower Richland High produced all of us, left indelible marks, and is our dear alma mater. We fought and loved and learned in that place, and though it was imperfect, many of us were mentored by teachers who genuinely wanted the best for us. Some of the alumni group members use the social media group to post queries in search of their favorite teachers, old flames, and long-lost close friends; others post to inform the group about the deaths or ill health of other alumni or to announce upcoming class gatherings and reunions.

Every once in a while, throw-away statements clue me in on what largely is not being said, particularly for those whose years at Lower Richland High were marked by a sense of terror or coming terror: a comment in a thread from the class of 1960-something in which someone mentions that a certain positive event that occurred during their matriculation was "before the school went downhill"; comments by a few participants that the upcoming reunion for the class of 1970-something was open to all and that everyone should come together, Black and white, and not maintain the segregated reunions of years prior. The group is not very active these days, but everyone is generally kind or silent in that "mind your manners" southern way. Yet school desegregation did a number on South Carolina and Lower Richland. Between parental fears and outward expressions of racism and abuse from adults, bullying, fights, and riots, it must have been a traumatic transition, most especially for the impressionable youth.

My mother was born in 1951 and attended one school for her entire K–12 career: the all-Black Webber School in Eastover, South Carolina. By the time her sister Gwen came along, Webber School was K–8, with the all-Black Hopkins High School as the secondary school option. It was the twins, Mike and Marie, who would be part of the cohort that would integrate Lower Richland High School in those tough early years. Everything that I know about Mike and Marie's time in high school (both passed away far too soon, Marie before I was born) centers around their Black Panther–inspired militant behavior while there. Their siblings recall them as black-pleatherwearing, good-intentioned hell raisers in the midst of desegregation.

School is perhaps the principal site in which we grow into social beings and begin thinking about political issues in a more independent way from our own parents. Mike and Marie's evolving political leanings were not embraced by Grandma Isabell, who had been an active member of nonviolent organizations in the 1960s, including the NAACP and the National Association of Colored Women. The ongoing education-related struggles across the country as well as the series of civil-rights-related assassinations in the 1960s no doubt made young Black people like my aunt and uncle curious about what a more direct, and perhaps even violent, response to racism and inequality might look like. Grandma often made trips to the school for one reason or another. Her twins were as spirited as she, though Grandma's beliefs aligned more with the principles of civil disobedience. Mike and Marie were the type of young people that many in my generation *swear* that they would have been, though I'm not so sure that any of us would have been as brave in the face of such racist intimidation.

In the early 1970s, hundreds of members of the Black Coalition for Justice voted to boycott Richland County schools until their demands for the guaranteed safety and fair treatment of Black students were met. Lower Richland High School and Dreher High School had been the sites of several fights between

Black and white students, leading to school closures and the placement of fifty police officers at Lower Richland High alone. The coalition argued about the school district's response to the unrest, "We cannot return to schools where hostility and inhumanity is not only continuing but has been further aggravated by the presence of police in the schools. . . . Education cannot take place in this dangerous emotional atmosphere" (Associated Press).

The Black Lower Richland High School parents were no doubt concerned about the ways that the discriminatory treatment of their children were being swept under the rug, especially as the Deadline '72 group organized to elect and succeeded in placing five conservative school board members to counter the progressive actions of M. Hayes Mizell, the white director of the South Carolina Community Relations Program of the American Friends Service Committee.

In an interview with Columbia, South Carolina's WIS-TV, Mizell explained that the unrest at Lower Richland was the result of a "clash of cultures and lifestyles" of people "thrown together for the first time" and that they needed to work together to make the transition easier for all. A devoted integrationist, Mizell was up against powerful forces that refused the idea that the "cultures" of Lower Richland could cease to clash.

Mizell had sat in on local community meetings with white parents who uttered that they did not wish to send their children to a "nigger school" and that they wanted to "stop this communist conspiracy" (Dufford 111). The Deadline '72 group appealed to white parents who opposed desegregation, by posting flyers to question whether they were "going to stand by, complacently, and let our schools be set back a hundred years." They appealed to white parents:

UNITE AND WIN
I LOVE MY CHILDREN
DO YOU LOVE YOURS? (Dufford 111)

Deadline '72 was led by the beloved, storied football coach Mooney Player, who felt that an "ultra-liberal element" wanted to control South Carolina's schools (Dufford 112). Between 1969 and 1971, Player was written up for physically assaulting Black students at Lower Richland High and fined in a magistrate court for his cruel behavior (111). But despite his abuses toward the children he was obligated to coach and protect, Player maintained his position at the school until he resigned in 1972. Buses, indeed, were the vehicles of integration—and of antagonism and danger too.

***

Some of my family members and acquaintances who were Lower Richland students during the height of the desegregation process have shared with me the horror of the time, the violence heaped on them and their friends, with the media sometimes laying the blame for instigating unrest at the feet of the Black teenagers. For these young African Americans to witness white parental love articulated through expressions of hatred and brutality no doubt affirmed to them that their futures—their chances at mobility—would be impaired by similar sentiments in professional spaces.

I know that Black parents in Lower Richland held their children up, became fixtures at schools and district offices, and did the best that they could to ensure that their progeny did not internalize white supremacist notions of Black inferiority. Perhaps they emoted similarly to James Baldwin in his carefully rendered letter to his nephew James in *The Fire Next Time*:

> If the word *integration* means anything, this is what it means, that we with love shall force our [white] brothers to see themselves as they are, to cease fleeing from reality and begin to change it, for this is your home, my friend. Do not be driven from it. Great men have done great things here and will again and we can make America what America must become. It will be hard, James, but you come from sturdy peasant stock, men who picked cotton, dammed rivers, built railroads, and in the teeth of the most terrifying odds, achieved an unassailable and monumental dignity. (9–10)

By the time I arrived at Lower Richland High two decades after desegregation, the school was still contending with the reputation it had been assigned during the early 1970s—it was viewed as a dangerous educational wasteland, and some parents transferred their children to other schools in the district. Those of us who remained often fell into cliques by race, an unfortunate verification of Black parents' worst fears—that forced busing and unmediated forced *intimacies* could not ensure true racial progress.

The South vigorously resisted busing and the desegregation of schools, yet it is now the most integrated region in the nation. As the past several decades have shown, however, busing itself was insufficient, as the practice was viewed as a direct threat to the white South's idea of itself. Without the passage of reparative educational legislation and the collective grappling with and accounting for painful histories, efforts to democratize our *union* will continue to fail. And given the dogged manner in which far too many Americans hold onto the power that white supremacy affords them in their personal, political, and professional lives, the promises of Black mobility have tended to forestall and sputter, leaving African Americans to negotiate uphill battles to ensure that their basic rights are recognized in the afterlife of slavery.

CODA

PASSAGES

During my junior year of college, I began a job as a part-time receptionist at a newly opened assisted-living facility in North Charleston. It was one of the best jobs I had as a college student not only because the administration made my life easy by refusing to allow my work duties to conflict too much with my need to study but also because the residents somehow made me feel closer to my Grandma Isabell, who by that time was living in a similar facility in Columbia due to her Alzheimer's diagnosis and my family's fear for her well-being. All but two residents were white people aged sixty or older, some with dementia or other ailments, while a few others were in good health but chose to reside there because they truly wanted to have the ease of retirement with twenty-four-hour medical care in-house, just in case, and a robust events calendar.

When I think back on that time, I smile remembering the fussy but harmless residents: those whose faces would light up when they saw me as they rounded the corner toward the dining room; the

Tuesday reveal of freshly coiffed female residents whose dyed, roller-set hair had taken on a light-blue tint and reminded me of the fluffiness of cotton candy; and the pair of women who only spoke with each other at length and considered themselves to be the best of friends. Like the roaming that Grandma Isabell and her buddy loved to do, these two women would often try to leave out the front door to go on a walk, one with her boxy black purse positioned on her forearm like Queen Elizabeth. I would lure them back with the promise of ice cream: "Ladies, we happen to have some delicious ice cream today if you would like some." And they would respond in a singsong southern lilt about that being *such* a good idea. It happened so often that I wondered if it weren't a ruse that the two had devised, but the sober part of me knew that it was their paired dementias that drove this confused, repetitive behavior. I was just pleased that through it all, they remembered their fondness for the sweet treat.

I became close to more than a few of these white elders during my two years there. The women in a feisty clique nicknamed me "Twiggy" after the famous British supermodel who, like me, was tall and lanky with large eyes and a page-boy haircut. My favorite resident was Mr. R——, a lovely man whom you would hear coming long before you saw him because of his oxygen tank. He was so pleasant that I could imagine him in better health sitting on the porch of his own home, inviting neighbors to sit for a while to enjoy a cool drink and chat. Born in the early twentieth century, these were all people who had lived through some of the most turbulent moments of South Carolina history. And perhaps they were on the wrong side of much of that history and had, at that moment in the late 1990s, found themselves at the edge of life, their lifelong concerns about race moderated by time or the fragility of their current circumstance.

The intimacies of the South have long been interesting to me because it is not unheard of to have a particular kind of closeness to people at school or on the job that never carries on outside of those spaces. I do not recall ever stepping foot in my white school friends' homes, and they did not visit mine either. At the assisted-living facility, though, we employees were basically at work in the residents' home. My job did not require that I engage them beyond perfunctory greetings and answering their general questions or concerns, but there I was nearly every single afternoon or evening shift laughing with members of various cliques, escorting residents to the nurses' station as needed, and singing songs with them during the music therapist's visits.

Mr. R—— was not at the facility long before he passed away. One afternoon, I received a panicked call from the head nurse, who said that Mr. R—— wanted to see me and that his time was short. I raced to work. When I arrived at the door to his room, I noticed that his children were there with a priest, who was preparing to deliver Mr. R—— his last rites. They waved me inside to join them in that sacred moment. Mr. R—— perked up when he saw me and recounted a prescient dream that he had had about me the evening before. I shook. Mr. R—— told me to continue to do well in school and that he loved me. I bent down closer to his bedside, and I choked out a whisper that I loved him too. He kissed my cheek. Then the priest began the rites.

As my graduation date approached, the residents and administration encouraged me to host my party there with them, and I agreed. My parents and many other family members made the trip from the Midlands. The residents who were able to give me a standing ovation did so as I walked into the dining room in my cap and gown. They were immensely happy that Twiggy from Lower Richland had finished college and was headed to graduate school at that. I hugged many of the residents' necks and collected cards of congratulation. We toasted with sweet tea and enjoyed the chef's special John's Island red rice and grilled chicken. The memory of this moment remains with me, heartens me. I praise the ways that some things have changed interpersonally back home, though I lament the racial hatred and acute levels of systemic inequality that remain.

The realization of an egalitarian America has been a long time coming. I will never affirm premature, mythic narratives of progress, as they belie the very real continuances and consequences of economic, educational, health, and social disparities in our times. For how many generations more must African Americans protest and shout to declare our humanity? This is truly a matter of life and breath.

* * *

New Light Beulah Baptist Church was my childhood place of worship. It was the church born out of the 1871 confrontation in which an armed Jesse Reese Adams holed himself up with his family to stop Black church members from taking ownership of the sanctuary they previously shared with Beulah Baptist Church. And in 2015, the church was on Dylann Roof's short list of churches to attack. He had been living in Lower Richland at the time. During his trial, it was revealed that Roof had conducted research about Black churches in South Carolina's Richland County and identified five possible targets for his murderous rampage. He later selected Charleston, in part because he had heard that the city had a large African American population. The potential for mass bloodshed and the creation of a lasting sense of terror appealed to Roof's depraved mind. So he traveled.

In the days after Roof gunned down parishioners at Mother Emanuel, newscasters and politicians alike applauded the surviving church members' forgiving posture. Their Christ-like grace, talk of unity, and refusal to politicize matters or blame white people publicly endeared them to a bipartisan group of Americans. Soon, political leaders from across the

South rushed to reconsider their states' embrace of Civil War iconography. We Americans, they insisted, are better than this. Southern politicians scrambled to approve and enforce new laws that saw to it that Confederate flags and other public memorials that are dedicated to slaveholders and the Lost Cause were removed and/or relocated to museums to prove that the myth of wholesale American progress was so.

The mass murder of God-fearing Black church congregants had shamed those who had theretofore remained too silent about the dangerous, racialized rhetoric that has marked the political conversation for ages. In response, these lawmakers guiltily and nervously moved to tear down the historical evidence.

But we should know by now that expressions of white guilt will never function as sustainable foundations on which to mount a truly progressive future. Often, such self-serving and belated recognitions of our shared humanity only follow what might come off as a submissive posture in the tamping down of Black rage in mixed company. This continued dance of submission, forgiveness, and guilt is not getting Black Americans anywhere.

Indeed, we are in the midst of an interminable bloody season. As I write now in 2020, Dylann Roof's attorneys have filed an appeal of his guilty conviction and death sentence, arguing that prosecutors should have never allowed him to represent himself, as he is a mentally ill man with a ninth-grade education. Roof has also initiated a hunger strike, citing incessant harassment and what he views as an unconscionable, blatant disregard for his life and well-being in prison.

Since Roof's 2015 rampage, Richland County alone has seen its share of disheartening flare-ups of white-supremacy in the rhetoric of and actions taken by young people. In 2018, Roof's eighteen-year-old sister, Morgan, made what many people viewed as a barely veiled threat against Black students at A. C. Flora High School who were prepared to join other activists for National Walkout Day, the event organized by survivors of the school shooting at Marjory Stoneman Douglas High School in Parkland, Florida, in which Nikolas Cruz murdered seventeen people. In response to the students' intentions to walkout, Morgan posted a video on Snapchat, stating, "I hope it's a trap and y'all get shot. We know it's fixing to be nothing but black people walkin out anyway." She was arrested later that same day for being in possession of weapons and marijuana on school grounds. In 2019, a white student at the private Cardinal Newman School was expelled and arrested for threatening to commit a mass atrocity as well. The unnamed sixteen-year-old shared a series of videos with his friends in which he brandished an automatic rifle and shotgun and uttered racist epithets, pretended to shoot Black people, and fired a gun repeatedly at a box containing Nike Jordan basketball sneakers. With all of the hatefulness in the state's past and present, South Carolina is one of four states that still does not have a hate crime law on the books.

In the 2010s alone, white domestic terrorists heaped violence on the unsuspecting at an alarming rate, but our elected officials did very little to curb the upsurge in outwardly expressed supremacism. Their collective failure to truly name racialized brutality for what it is along with their lack of courage to work earnestly to defeat it renders complicit each one of them, whose sole actions are stale, pedestrian utterances of regret in the aftermath. No American should be wholly surprised by such disturbances occurring in our public spaces in such rapid succession. We had every indication of this possibility.

Take, for instance, President Trump's now-infamous question from the campaign trail in 2016: "What do [African Americans] have to lose.... What the hell do you [African Americans] have to lose?" Trump's spectacle was an affected performance of a "tell it like it is" posture before a nearly all white audience; as he feigned a desire to win the Black vote, Trump sarcastically rattled off a list of what he deemed to be African American failures, including the community's supposed naive faithfulness to the Democratic Party. With a mocking tone, Trump connected Blackness to inherent deficiency, offering a thinly veiled reinforcement to his base that the Trump-Pence ticket subscribed to the notion that somehow African Americans are pathologically irresponsible, impoverished because of their own laziness and lack of grit, and owners of nothing from which it would hurt them to part. The most significant extrapolation from this particular ahistorical dog whistle and the Trump administration's ensuing contemptible actions, even in the midst of a pandemic, is this: Black people's bodies are the sites on which anything can and will continue to occur unabated in the name of upholding white supremacy. History tells us that this is so.

Whither justice in a land of barbarous white supremacists who thrive on our blood and tears? When there is continued indifference to the vulnerability of Black life in America, when we are perceived firstly as threats to be silenced permanently rather than precious human lives, we rage and mourn but also endeavor to imagine new possibilities for survival.

Ours is a legacy of creative and persistent agitation against any ideal that forecloses the possibility of Black freedom and mobility. The perpetuity of injustice is why we would do well to never stop dreaming of the kind of place to which we might travel to truly make a life.

But where in the world can we go? What kinds of new spaces of passage can we fight to create right here? This is urgent. It has always been urgent. We have everything to lose.

Acknowledgments

I have been thinking about this book for several years now and Lower Richland, South Carolina, certainly, for my entire life. In my work and in my personal life, I am infatuated by the promises of flight. The long history of brutality and undue restrictions on Black lives incenses me, and so I endeavor to trace these ceaseless threats on Black mobility. I marvel at narratives of resistance and stand in awe of Black people's movements over/across/through the wilderness.

Thank you to the fantastic Avidly Reads series editors, Sarah Blackwood and Sarah Mesle, for their support of my ideas for this book and for their patience with me as I researched and drafted the manuscript. They helped me shape the narrative and organize the many pieces, always eager and always excited about my work. Sincere appreciation to the entire team at NYU Press for their enthusiasm and commitment to this project, especially those I worked with most closely: Eric Zinner, Dolma Ombadykow, and Martin Coleman.

My friend Margaret Lazarus Dean gave me good writing advice and read the manuscript with care. I cannot thank her enough. My other dear friends and colleagues are far too many to name here, though I deeply appreciate their encouragement and belief in my ability to tell this story.

To my ancestral and living family members, known and unknown, I love you. I am grateful for the sacrifices that you made to make my life possible. I know it was not easy. For what you endured and triumphed over, for what you endure and triumph over, I give reverence. I hope that I've done well by you in recounting these stories of passage.

Bibliography

Adams, Edward C. L. *Tales of the Congaree*. Edited by Robert G. O'Meally. Chapel Hill: University of North Carolina Press, 1987.

Associated Press. "Many Blacks Boycott Columbia Schools." *Index-Journal*, March 13, 1972, 9.

Baker, J. A. "Address by John A. Baker, Assistant Secretary, U.S. Department of Agriculture, at Ohio State Resource Development Conference, Columbus, Ohio, Friday, March 29, 1968, 10:15 a.m. (CST)." https://archive.org/CAT31380717?.

Baldwin, James. "My Dungeon Shook." *The Fire Next Time*, 1–10, 1963. New York: Vintage, 1993.

Best, Jeryl, and Arthur Stanley. "Jeryl Best and Arthur Stanley on Lamar Violence—Outtakes." Interview. WIS-TV News Story 70-354. March 3, 1970. https://mirc.sc.edu.

Brevard, Keziah. *A Plantation Mistress on the Eve of the Civil War: The Diary of Keziah Goodwyn Hopkins Brevard, 1860–1861*. Columbia: University of South Carolina Press, 1993.

Bryant, Bobby. "Senate Saluting 'Forgotten' Victims of 1970 Lamar Riots." *News & Press* (Darlington, SC), April 30, 2019. www.newsandpress.net.

Camp, Stephanie M. H. *Closer to Freedom: Enslaved Women and Everyday Resistance in the Plantation South*. Chapel Hill: University of North Carolina Press, 2005.

Congaree National Park South Carolina. "Home of Champions." Accessed November 7, 2019. www.nps.gov.

Craft, William. *Running a Thousand Miles for Freedom*. 1860. New York: Dover, 2014.

Dent, Harry. "Dent on Lamar Violence—Outtakes." Interview. WIS-TV News Story 70-374 (A). March 7, 1970. https://mirc.sc.edu.

Douglass, Frederick. *Narrative of the Life of Frederick Douglass, An American Slave*. 1845. New York: Modern Library, 2000.

———. "Why Should a Colored Man Enlist?" *Douglass' Monthly*, April 1863. https://rbscp.lib.rochester.edu.

Du Bois, W. E. B. "Returning Soldiers." *Crisis* 18 (May 1919): 13–14.

Dufford, William E. *My Tour through the Asylum: A Southern Integrationist's Memoir*. Columbia: University of South Carolina Press, 2017.

Equiano, Olaudah. *The Interesting Narrative of the Life of Olaudah Equiano; or, Gustavus Vassa, the African*. 1789. New York: Modern Library, 2004.

Facing History and Ourselves. "South Carolina 'Red Shirts' Battle Plan." 1876. Accessed December 20, 2019. www.facinghistory.org.

Falconbridge, Alexander. *An Account of the Slave Trade on the Coast of Africa by Alexander Falconbridge, Late Surgeon in the African Trade*. London: J. Phillips, 1788.

"Ford Foundation to Back High-Risk Social Ventures." *Corpus Christi Caller-Times*, September 29, 1968, 3.

"Frank Threatt's Quiet Drive on Prejudice." *Life*, December 15, 1967.

Hughes, Langston. *I Wonder as I Wander: An Autobiographical Journey*. New York: Hill and Wang, 1993.

"Lamar Riot Trial—Outtakes." Newscast. WIS-TV News Story 71-171. February 17, 1971. https://mirc.sc.edu.

Lawson, John. *A New Voyage to Carolina; Containing the Exact Description and Natural History of the*

Country: Together with the Present State Thereof. London, 1709.

Lockley, Timothy James, ed. *Maroon Communities in South Carolina: A Documentary Record*. Columbia: University of South Carolina Press, 2009.

McIllwain, William F. "On the Overturning of Two School Buses in Lamar, SC." *Esquire*, April 1, 1971. https://classic.esquire.com/.

Mizell, M. Hayes. Interview. WIS-TV News Story, May 5, 1972. https://mirc.sc.edu.

Morrison, Toni. *Beloved*. 1987. New York: Vintage, 2004.

Ross, William O., and Duke L. Slaughter. *With the 351st in France (A Diary)*. Baltimore: Afro-American Company, [1919?].

Sharpe, Christina. *In the Wake: On Blackness and Being*. Durham, NC: Duke University Press, 2016.

Siemsen, Thora. "On Working with Archives: An Interview with Writer Saidiya Hartman." *Creative Independent*, April 18, 2018. https://thecreativeindependent.com/.

Smallwood, Stephanie E. *Saltwater Slavery: A Middle Passage from Africa to African Diaspora*. Cambridge, MA: Harvard University Press, 2008.

Smithsonian National Postal Museum. "1898 Postmaster Lynching." *Behind the Badge: The US Postal Inspection Service*. Exhibition. Accessed December 20, 2019. https://postalmuseum.si.edu/.

South Carolina. Act for the Better Ordering and Governing Negroes and Other Slaves in This Province. Slave Code of South Carolina. May 1740. https://digital.scetv.org/.

South Carolina Education Survey Committee. *Public Schools of South Carolina: A Report of the South Carolina Education Survey Committee*. Nashville, TN: Division of Surveys and Field Services, George Peabody College for Teachers, 1948.

Stroyer, Jacob. *My Life in the South*. 3rd ed. Salem, MA: Salem Observer, 1885.

Thurmond, Strom. "Address of Senator Strom Thurmond (D-SC) on Political Motivations of Civil Rights Legislation and Northern versus Southern System of Segregation on Senate Floor, April 1, 1960." Strom Thurmond Collection, Mss. 100.2040. https://tigerprints.clemson.edu.

US Congress. *Rural Renewal: Hearings before the Subcommittee on Financing and Investment of the Select Committee on Small Business, United States Senate, Ninetieth Congress, Second Session, on Small Business Development and Rural Renewal, May 23 and June 27, 1968*. Washington, DC: US Government Printing Office, 1968.

US Department of Labor. *The Economic Situation of Negroes in the United States*. Washington, DC: US Department of Labor, 1962.

Williams, John A. *This Is My Country Too*. New York: Signet, 1966.

About the Author

Michelle D. Commander is Associate Director and Curator of the Lapidus Center for the Historical Analysis of Transatlantic Slavery at the Schomburg Center for Research in Black Culture. Previously, Commander was a tenured Associate Professor of English and Africana Studies at the University of Tennessee, Knoxville. A Ford Foundation fellow and Fulbright grant recipient, she is the author of *Afro-Atlantic Flight: Speculative Returns and the Black Fantastic* and editor of *Unsung: Unheralded Narratives of American Slavery & Abolition.*

www.ingramcontent.com/pod-product-compliance
Lightning Source LLC
Chambersburg PA
CBHW052039070526
44584CB00020B/3168